Adva

Peace of the City: A Handbook for Missional Communities

This book offers a prophetic invitation to lean into the uncomfortable. Real-life examples intrigue the heart. Deep wisdom stirs the mind. But the unmistakable summons of the Prince of Peace will change everything. Come and see!

—John H. Bouwers
Entrepreneur, church planter
Leader of the Church Planting Institute, CRCNA

If you have ever asked yourself, *What might this look like?* or *Where would I start?* then Terence has something valuable to offer you. This book offers the reader genuinely practical step-by-step advice on what it looks like to lead a community on mission in Canada.

—Jared Siebert
National Director of Church Development
Free Methodist Church in Canada

Beyond the principles of this handbook, the heart and themes of the book articulate the faithful pilgrimage of a community on mission.

—Jesse Sudirgo
Tyndale professor and Director of the Church in the City
Masters of Divinity Program

Terence combines the theory of mission with personal experience and biblical story to give inspiration, insight, and helpful instruction to anyone interested in living a more missional life.

—Marian Lensink
Resonate Global Mission

In *Peace of the City*, Terence Schilstra has wrestled with theology, missiology, sense of place, and the practice of ministry in the real-time lab of The Table. I commend his insights for all ministry practitioners seeking light in these dim times.

—Dan Sheffield
Pastor, church planter, author
and adjunct lecturer at Tyndale Seminary

Joining God on mission is the calling of every Christ follower since the early church. *Peace in the City* is a practical and easy-to-follow guide of what that journey of following Christ can look like. A must-read for everyone wanting to engage in Christ's mission right in your own neighbourhood.

—Michael Collins
Church planter and mission catalyst

Intentional and passionate. These are the words that come to mind as I read Terence Schilstra's book, *Peace of the City*. Terence has proven the content of this book by his actions in downtown Thorold. At a time in history when the church needs to pivot about the why and how of being the church, *Peace of the City* is a place to go to imagine, dream, and pray. The book is a measuring tool of understanding that we need God, ourselves, and our neighbours to model what Christ modelled to us. It is a book that will help to challenge thinking and provide practical steps of what it means to live in missional community. Well done.

—Beth Fellinger
Church planter and Regional Mission Leader for Resonate
Eastern Canada

Peace of the City: A Handbook for Missional Communities invites you into a story of God's transforming peace in the actual, real-life situations of a small-group-turned-missional-community in Thorold, Ontario. This book doesn't just present a conceptual or espoused theology of the authentic Christian life in our communities; it is embodied in the life that tells the story. Terence creatively explores a selection of core practices and rhythms that offer guidance to anyone seeking to cultivate authentic missional living. I will recommend this to any Christian seeking to be challenged to grow in love for the people and communities into which God has called them to serve faithfully and selflessly.

—Jervis Djokoto
Executive Director, The Renew Movement

What I most appreciate about this book is that it is so practical; you can put the principles into practice in your own setting. I have known Terence Schilstra and worked in ministry with him for over ten years. Terence lives out this book in daily ministry in his context in downtown Thorold. Read the book, be inspired, and then go and live it out!

—Hilda Vanderklippe
Missional Leader at The Village Church

Peace

of the City

**A Handbook
for Missional Communities**

Terence Schilstra

PEACE OF THE CITY
Copyright © 2021 by Terence Schilstra

Printed in Canada

Print ISBN: 978-1-4866-2100-2
eBook ISBN: 978-1-4866-2101-9

Word Alive Press
119 De Baets Street, Winnipeg, MB R2J 3R9
www.wordalivepress.ca

Cataloguing in Publication may be obtained through Library and Archives Canada

Contents

Preface   xiii

Definitions   xv

Introduction   xix

The Mission of the King: The Author of Peace   xxi

Part One: The Missional Community: Growing Out   1

Part Two: The Missional Community: Growing In   21

Part Three: The Missional Community: Growing Up   33

Part Four: The Christian Life   49

Part Five: Missional Leadership   61

Part Six: Missional Community Structures   73

Community Profile   77

Bibliography   85

About the Author   91

For Karen, Noah, Autumn, Ashley, and Joe
who continue to teach me the true meaning of love.

All the profits of this book go directly towards the ministry of The Table and the ongoing positive transformation of Downtown Thorold.

To learn more, please visit peaceofthecity.ca, or contact Terence Schilstra at peaceofthecity.book@gmail.com.

Preface

A few years ago, seven average Christians from our church started meeting every other Sunday evening to explore God's Word and pray together in an intentional small group. As we met together, our small group deepened our relationship with God and got to know each other a little better. After a year of meeting, someone suggested we start eating together regularly. Quickly enough, the meal table became central to our rhythm as a group.

Over time, we felt God inviting us to expand that table to include our unbelieving neighbours. By the end of the next year, we had hosted our first community dinner at an inner-city school in downtown Thorold. After five years, our missional community had grown to more than twenty Christians and connected with about thirty families in our community.

At our community dinners, we began averaging between forty and sixty people. We started to deepen relationships with our neighbours, and through the work of God we saw people come to Christ and be baptized. Furthermore, we saw our neighbourhood transformed in amazing ways.

This book is the story of how God transformed a small Bible study group into a missional community with a heart to make a big difference in our neighbourhood. More than that, this story brims with hope for how we might further cultivate our faith and live it out in the crucible of our community.

I offer this book primarily as a gift to our missional community, to help us grow in Christ and challenge us towards missional engagement and leadership. Yet I've also written this book as a discipleship resource, to inform new Christians who have connected with our missional community, to invite them into a biblical model of life and community.

Additionally, my prayer is that this book would cultivate the missional imagination of other small groups, missional communities, and churches throughout our region, province, country, and beyond. Whoever reads this book, here's my challenge: find *one* thing in this book that makes you feel uncomfortable and lean into it. Indeed, every great journey starts by taking one brave step into the unknown.

Definitions

What is a missional community?

A missional community is a group of people who actively participate in God's mission to engage God's world, according to his Word. A missional community is neither a program nor an inward-focused small group; it is a movement of regular Christians living out God's mission in their community.

Fundamentally, our mission, as the great missional thinker Christopher Wright declares, "is the committed participation as God's people, at God's invitation and command, in God's own mission within the history of God's world for the redemption of God's creation through Christ."[1]

As a people who carry the mission of God in our DNA, we are sent by God to live on mission in our neighbourhoods. Missional communities, therefore, live an intentional lifestyle of repeated actions, growing in intensity as they participate in the mission of God within their orbit.

---

1   J.H. Christopher Wright, *The Mission of God: Unlocking the Bible's Grand Narrative* (Downers Grove, IL: InterVarsity Press, 2006), 23.

How do missional communities affect their community?

Missional people acknowledge that every personal relationship and encounter in their stomping grounds is an opportunity to share the love of Jesus Christ with words and actions.

Words. Missiologist Jeff Vanderstelt says that missional communities "speak the truths of Jesus into the everyday stuff of life"[2] so that the peace of Christ overflows into our everyday interactions and conversations.

Actions. Additionally, missional communities are attentive to how God wants us to work in his world. The Bible says, *"For we are God's handiwork, created in Christ Jesus to do good works, which God prepared in advance for us to do"* (Ephesians 2:10). In every opportunity, missional communities live worthy of the calling they have received to be ambassadors of Jesus Christ, participating in God's mission to bring love, peace, and hope into their orbit through a community of missional practices and postures.

What does "missional" mean?

For at least the last hundred years of the church, missions have been recognized as a branch of the church. Accordingly, faith communities historically sent missionaries[3] overseas, the likes of which have included Hudson Taylor and William Carey, to places with a particular mandate: "to convert unbelievers."[4] Thus, missionary activity has been associated with bringing the gospel "to the beyond."

This missional branch of the church was rooted mostly in one verse of the Bible: the great commission in Matthew 28:19, which advises us, *"Therefore go and make disciples of all nations…"* This form of "going" was a contextual conclusion of the day which

---

2   Jeff Vanderstelt, *Gospel Fluency* (Wheaton, IL: Crossway, 2017), 3.

3   Overseas missions are still, of course, an essential task today.

4   Wright, *The Mission of God*, 34.

deduced, "We are all Christians here in the West, but the rest of the nations still need to hear the gospel, so let's send missionaries to go to these places."

Today, however, we live in a Western society that is far from Christian. In fact, much of Canada's population would describe themselves as non-religious[5] or not Christian at all. Thus, the church has had to redefine "mission" in fresh terms. The church today widely agrees that we are standing in a new mission field in the West: our own neighbourhoods.

With this reality in view, even our conception of God revealed in Scripture is making a positive shift. We are now beginning to realize that God does not merely call the church to send various missionaries into the borderlands. Rather, we see God as a missionary in all time and space. Accordingly, mission is not just a random denominational branch of the church; God himself is missional in nature.

Further, mission in Scripture is not limited to one phrase in Matthew 28. Instead Scripture is a missional phenomenon in and of itself.[6] Therefore, because both God and Scripture are missional in nature, so too is the community of God called to be missional. Thus, we are called to be missional communities.

---

5   James Watson, *Religious Nones: A Growing Trend*, New Leaf. April 22, 2017 (https://newleafnetwork.squarespace.com/articles/religious-nones-growing-trend).

6   Wright, *The Mission of God*, 34.

Introduction

There once was a king who offered a prize to the artist who could paint the best picture of peace. Many artists tried. The king looked at all the pictures, but there were only two that really caught his eye.

One picture was of a beautiful peaceful city. The city was perfectly calm, with tall buildings in the background. Overhead was a perfect blue sky with cotton ball clouds. All who looked at the picture thought that it was a perfect picture of peace.

The other picture had tall buildings too. But these were tired and rugged. Above was an angry sky from which rain fell and lightning crashed. The streets between the buildings tumbled and foamed with traffic and pedestrians. This did not look peaceful at all. But when the king looked, he saw tucked in an alley a young mom under an umbrella. There, in the midst of the wet, rusty buildings and angry cars, she sat calmly with her three children… in perfect peace.

The king chose the second picture. His kingdom was in shock.

On the day he awarded the prize, he declared, "I chose this painting because peace does not mean there is no noise, trouble, or pain. Peace is what it means to be in the midst of all those things and still be calm in your heart. That is the real meaning of peace."

Peace. The ancient Hebrews had a word for peace: shalom (שלום). The meaning of the word is: wholeness, to be complete. Shalom is perfect peace, "the way things ought to be."[7] The key dimension of shalom is a state of being. Shalom is like the young mom sitting peacefully under the umbrella. Shalom is perfect and complete wholeness in heart, mind, body, and soul, even amid the mania of life.

Pause for a minute. Close your eyes. Slow down your breathing. Let your body relax. Lower your shoulders. Clear your mind.

Shalom.

Peace is a state of being, but it is also active. We can pursue shalom. If there is a conflict within our orbit, we can work towards a peaceful resolution.

This morning as I walked down the stairs towards our kitchen table, my peace was shattered by the sound of our four young children squabbling over who was going to pour the orange juice for breakfast. I could have sat down at the table and waited for peace to arrive amid the squabble. Instead I pursued peace. I calmly sat and asked the kids how we could resolve the situation. Peace was negotiated. We prayed together and ate in peace, sharing stories and laughing together.

In a similar fashion, shalom can be pursued in our relationships, work, and neighbourhoods.

Peace is indeed an attainable state of being—and it is active. Yet the true criterion for peace rests outside of ourselves. The fact is that genuine peace comes to us and our community by way of experiencing the author and perfecter of peace.

---

7   Cornelius Plantinga Jr., *Not the Way It's Supposed to Be: A Breviary of Sin* (Grand Rapids, MI: Eerdmans, 1995), 10.

The Mission of the King: The Author of Peace

At the beginning of time, a loving King created a perfect world (Genesis 1, John 1). His kingdom and everything in it was characterized by one Hebrew word: *shalom*. Peace.

The earth was full of shalom, the kind of peace in which everything works according to the King's good intentions. Indeed, there was perfect harmony in the kingdom between the King, his people, and creation. However, in the time of peace, the King's crown jewel, man and woman (Adam and Eve), rebelled. They disobeyed the King. That rebellion resulted in their physical death. Peace was shattered. Since then, shards of that rebellion have constantly stabbed into the heart of humanity.

Nevertheless, the loving King determined to turn this dark event that humans caused into good that would be to his ultimate glory. Even though humanity rebelled, the great and loving King pursued peace to make his enemies his friends. The good King implemented a master plan to bring peace back to his kingdom.

The King initiated the plan by entering into a relationship with a people who would become a people of shalom: the nation Israel. They would be the King's chosen people to represent peace in the world. He formed them as a nation. He gave them a promised land. In that land, the King provided them everything they needed to live and thrive in harmony—everything the King intended community and a neighbourhood to be.

However, after a season, the nation Israel's people rebelled against each other and against the good King. The shards of the rebellion ran deep, perpetuated by Satan himself. Peace was shattered once more.

The King was sad that his people had rejected his love yet again, but he again turned this rebellion into his glory. The King brought forth perfect peace from rebel Israel.

From the line of Israel, the King sent his Son Jesus. From an Israelite virgin, the baby Jesus was born. He was human, yet fully God (John 1:1). Angels heralded his arrival: "Glory to the newborn King! Peace on earth and mercy mild, God and rebels reconciled."

As the Son of the King grew in age and stature, he declared, "I have been sent by my Father the King to usher in a new kingdom: *shalom.*"[8]

Jesus *is* the shalom. The Bible proclaims, *"For he himself is our peace..."* (Ephesians 2:14). His life and presence are the marks of a new kingdom order of peace for our lives and our neighbourhoods.

The perfect peace that Jesus brings, however, comes at a cost. After all, peace is active.

Jesus brought shalom through his life, but also through his painful death. In an amazing act of love for his people, Jesus laid down his life on a cross to conquer the effects of sin and rebellion. He was crucified, died, and was buried.

The hope of peace seemed to be lost in his death. Yet in an astonishing reversal, Jesus's death removed the stabbing shards of the rebellion. His death in humanity's place satisfied the perfect justice of the King.

---

8   See Luke 4:44 and Matthew 4:17.

Herein is the gospel, the good news that the King accomplishes our salvation for us through Jesus Christ in order to bring us into a right relationship with him.[9] Thus, Jesus' costly act of putting on the robes of humanity and stepping into our place before God accomplished the gift of complete redemption and restoration.[10] Perfection. Wholeness. Peace. The Bible declares, "Jesus, who had no sin, became sin for us so that in him we might become reunited as children of the King."[11]

In another stunning turn of events, three days after Jesus's death and burial, he rose from the dead and appeared once more in his community to declare, *"Peace be with you! As the Father has sent me, I am sending you"* (John 20:21). Yes, the King raised his Son back to life, thereby conquering death. He actively crushed the sting of mortality. Indeed, the prospect of humanity's eternal perishing was swallowed up by Jesus' victory over the grave (1 Corinthians 15:54–55). We can have eternal life and perfect immortality because of Jesus.

After Jesus' resurrection, he tore down the barrier between earth and heaven. All those who love him and place their faith in him will now live forever. He has paved a way for us to return to the King.

On the way up the ladder to heaven after his resurrection, our Saviour declared, "I am going to heaven to prepare a perfect place for you." A place of everlasting and true unending peace.

Jesus departed.

Yet as a sign and seal of that eternal peace, the sovereign King sent his very own Spirit to live in the hearts, minds, souls, and bodies of all those who place their faith in the finished work

9   Tim Keller, *Center Church* (Grand Rapids, MI: Zondervan, 2012), 31.

10   Reggie L. Williams, *Black Jesus: Harlem Renaissance Theology and an Ethic of Resistance* (Waco, TX: Baylor University Press, 2014), 200.

11   Paraphrased from 2 Corinthians 5:21.

of Jesus. The Spirit of shalom is on us! Thus, the Spirit carries us through the trials of life and death and back to God our Creator-King for eternity.

Although the rebellion will rage on earth until Jesus' return, the age of the Spirit of Jesus reigns today. We live in the age of spiritual peace.

Yes, the world remains rusty and broken. Sin still exists in our community. Satan still destroys. The physical body still dies. But through the Spirit of Jesus, who is our peace, there is victory and we have become a new creation. Our old spirit is gone; the new spirit is here. Perfect peace and rest have been achieved. We've become the peace of God. Therefore, as members of the church or missional community we have become ambassadors of peace in our world.

Part One

The Missional Community: Growing Out

ON A COLD SUNDAY EVENING IN DOWNTOWN THOROLD, A young couple and their two girls walked into a convenience store. The mom held up her sagging jogging pants with one hand while she picked out dinner: four hotdogs from the rolling warming rack. The dad's hoodie was pulled up over his head so no one would recognize him; he was on the run from his enemies. He nervously scanned the aisles as their daughters drooled over the selection of candy bars.

They met up at the checkout counter, right next to where they sold the slushies. Mom tried to pay for the hotdogs with her debit card, but the machine flashed a message saying she had insufficient funds. Dad wrangled around in his pockets for change—empty.

As they walked back to their apartment, ashamed, stomachs growling, their hearts felt like their financial state, empty and insufficient. Mom, holding her sagging pants, worried about when they would get enough money to feed their girls. Dad's mind raced anxiously, wondering how his family would manage while he was serving weekends in jail.

They were three months behind on rent, so on the way back to their apartment they ducked under their superintendent's window. As they slithered through the thickness of the evening, they saw in the distance silhouettes slipping into the open door of an inner-city school. The family then changed direction and walked towards the light, the girls following behind Mom and Dad while inadvertently scratching bedbug bites.

Suddenly, the smell of dinner caught their nose.

They peeked inside the school door only to be welcomed by our missional community and invited to stay for a meal. There they met new people and ate their fill. To their surprise, this gathering had been organized by a Christian group called a "missional community."

The next week, they came again. Over time, they formed friendships. They found belonging. They experienced love. They joined a missional community. They learned to pray and worship. They heard the story of the King of peace. They found peace!

Sometime later, at a gathering around the table, the mom declared, "Ever since that day when we first walked into this community, our lives have been changed."

She went on to describe feeling a renewed wholeness in her life. She also explained the peace her family was experiencing.

In time, the family came to know the story of Jesus. They gave their lives to him, responding to his restorative love. Jesus took away the insufficiency in their hearts and replaced it with peace, just as Jesus promised in the Bible: *"Come to me, all of you who are weary and carry heavy burdens, and I will give you rest"* (Matthew 11:28, NLT).

Today, there are still months when they cannot pay rent, and days when cockroaches parade through their living room, days when they cannot afford convenience store hotdogs. However, inwardly they found relief. Outwardly, they found the love and care of Jesus in community.

Communities of Missional Practice

Missional communities participate in God's mission to bring love, peace, and hope into their orbit through missional practices and postures. We live out these missional practices in such a way that they touch the people in our neighbourhoods. For our missional community, we have engaged with the urban poor in the inner city.

This section of the book will seek to cultivate the imagination of missional communities towards the goal of "growing out" together to love their neighbours in the name of Jesus.

As we have engaged with our neighbours, we have prayerfully enacted the following biblical practices.

1. Radical hospitality. The core practice of our missional community has been sharing a table with those community members whom God has called us to love. In particular, we feel called to share meals with individuals and families who live on the margins and in social isolation. Our desire is to follow Jesus' example by breaking bread with the outcasts of society and to love and engage them meaningfully (Mark 2:15, John 13:2, Luke 22:14, Luke 19:5).

As our missional community has continued to grow, we have shared meals in a variety of places, including in community centres, schools, parks, and homes, with lots of space for creativity. As we eat together, we intentionally create a welcoming and comfortable atmosphere where relationships and peace can flourish.

As relationships are nurtured, we desire to see people's lives *and* our community transformed.[12] The benchmarks that delineate transformation may include, but are not limited to:

---

12   Robert Linthicum, *City of God; City of Satan* (Grand Rapids, MI: Zondervan, 1991), Kindle location 1390.

1. People who were once isolated find connection and belonging in community.
2. Families and neighbours who were divided are given the opportunity to experience relational peace as they share a meal together.
3. Those who cannot always afford a meal are blessed by the gift of the shared meal.
4. New friendships are cultivated.

Historic missional communities, such as Benedictine and Franciscan communities, were archetypal for sharing the table of radical hospitality. Their gatherings were always filled with guests and strangers,[13] their tables constantly surrounded by community members who were invited to eat and share a meal.[14]

It's interesting to note that the "rules" outlining the practices of the Benedictine and Franciscan communities did *not* intentionally promote a requirement for hospitality. Rather, radical hospitality was central to their way of life. It was the air they breathed.

They measured radical hospitality not by varieties of bread or extravagances on the table. Instead they embodied hospitality by the ways in which they treated and served their guests. Anyone was welcome: the poor, the stranger, the outcast, and those who didn't look like them. Indeed, authentic hospitality is always focused on welcoming the guest, not the spread of food.

The love and humility shown to our neighbours will always be remembered over the taste of the meal. Our goal is not the spread, but the opportunity to show the love of Jesus at the table. The meal needs no saviour. So we focus on loving and serving people in the name of Christ.

---

13   Benedict of Nursia, *The Rule of St. Benedict,* trans. Boniface Verheyen, 1949, lvi.

14   Ibid.

Practically speaking, our missional community gatherings, worship, and Bible studies will include a meal around a table. At those gatherings, we'll always invite and include our unbelieving neighbours.

For instance, recently our missional community hosted a teaching series on the life of Jesus, each of these gatherings centred around the table of radical hospitality so that the love of Jesus could be shared and embodied. As we made plans, we invited our neighbours to eat with us and explore questions about Jesus and his life.

The diversity of neighbours who came, and continue to come, is amazing! A single woman who's been a shut-in for years comes out. A Muslim couple consistently comes as well because they love contributing to the meals, connecting with community, and learning about Jesus. A married couple, professed atheists, come with their four young children. There's a convicted criminal who enjoys the sense of belonging he gets. Two Asian women come along with their blended family. We also host those who are physically disabled.

In each case, our neighbours experience belonging and peace at the table of hospitality, regardless of who they are.

Furthermore, in our personal lives, we are encouraged to share a meal with each other and our neighbours at least once a month.

A great example of this is a couple I greatly respect who leads a missional community in a neighbouring city. They have had a young man over for dinner every week for the last five years and have shared amazing stories of their faithful service. He is from a broken, single-parent home; Dad is out of the picture. Yet amid the brokenness, my friends usher in peace by making the mundane drive to pick this lad up across town every week and bring him to their home for dinner.

They've developed a deep relationship with him and in the process have seen his life take shape. He's found peace in certain areas of life as they've prayed with, and for him, consistently.

Nevertheless, after all these years, there has not been any noticeable spiritual transformation in the young man's life. But that is the beauty of the story! This couple has felt called by God to love this neighbour and serve him at the table of radical hospitality—and that is exactly what they have done.

Missional hospitality means being committed to serving the other, regardless of whether a neighbour comes to faith in Christ. As we share meals with our neighbours and develop relationships, our motives within these relationships must not be *ulterior*. That is, we will not befriend these individuals with the intention to "fix" their lives or make them into new converts.

In *The Art of Neighboring*, authors Jay Pathak and Dave Runyon remind us, "The 'agenda' we need to drop is this well-meaning tendency to be friends with people for the sole purpose of converting them to our faith."[15] Rather, we do so because we love them and are genuinely interested in journeying through life together.

That said, as we eat together, the missional community is, of course, encouraged to have spiritual conversations with those whom we are connecting. This Spirit-filled dialogue may include sharing a Bible story before or after a meal. It may include respectfully asking to pray in the name of Jesus with our new friends at mealtime. It might involve casually sharing one's own faith story or asking questions about personal faith. Thus, we lean into opportunities to share and hear the gospel.

In summary, sharing the table of radical hospitality must be part of the DNA of our missional community. We must be sure to include the stranger, the widow, and the orphan at the

---

15   Jay Pathak and Dave Runyon, *The Art of Neighboring* (Grand Rapids, MI: Baker Books, 2012), 102.

table; the kingdom of God belongs to such as these. When offering hospitality, regard these words of Jesus: *"But when you give a banquet, invite the poor, the crippled, the lame, the blind, and you will be blessed. Although they cannot repay you, you will be repaid at the resurrection of the righteous"* (Luke 14:13–14).

2. Caring for the poor and powerless. Missional communities will love and protect the poor and powerless. The Christian communities of Benedict Nusia and Francis of Asisi have etched their names in history as stalwarts committed to serving the weak. Benedict declares, "Above all let care be scrupulously shewn in receiving the poor and strangers."[16] The Benedictines were prolific in their response to caring for the hundreds of weak and poor gripped by famine and plague in the wake of the Roman Empire's collapse (476 CE). From that moment in history, they earned renown for their deep devotion to providing physical, mental, and spiritual care to the least of these in their community.

Similarly, in the 1200s Francis of Asisi challenged his missional community to commit their working wage to the poor. Throughout the history of the church, Franciscan orders have worked tirelessly in their neighbourhoods, collecting money and food for the poor in their city. In fact, they intentionally moved into poor urban centres to care for the marginalized. The Franciscan rule evokes images of Christians on mission, working alongside struggling members of the community to help them collect and prepare food from the fields. In essence, they gave up their lives to serve the least of these.

In the same way, missional communities will inhabit poverty and brokenness in their neighbourhood. They will move in to live and work among the poor. They will be intentional in discussing the lot of the weak, poor, and powerless. They will prayerfully discern how God is calling them to respond to these challenges.

---

16   Benedict of Nursia, *The Rule of St. Benedict*, liii.

Practically speaking, for my friends, Patt and Gwenn, caring for the poor and weak meant sacrificing their lifestyle to take orphans into their homes. With another friend, it meant giving up her peaceful job in a perfect school to take a teaching job in a troubled inner-city school.

Personally, our family sold our home to live among the urban poor. For the last number of years, I have mentored at-risk kids in downtown Thorold. As I have been present in these kids' orbit, I've seen the peace of Christ break into their lives in beautiful ways. In particular, I have been mentoring a boy with severe anger issues and seen amazing progress in his life over the last two years. My prayer is that this emotional change will usher peace into his life and have a positive impact on other members of his own family.

In *Letters and Papers from Prison*, Bonhoeffer reminds us, "[Jesus Christ was] weak and powerless in the world, and that is precisely the way, the only way, in which he is with us and helps us."[17] In other words, Christ steps into our humanity to join us in our poor and weak state. As far as Christ lived and died in vicarious weakness, Bonhoeffer argued that so too are his disciples (that's us) called to vicariously suffer with and for others.[18]

Simply put, missional communities adjust their lifestyle to love and care for those who are most obviously in need in their community. Church father Gregory of Nazianzus believed that "caring for the poor and weak, sacrificing oneself for their

17 Dietrich Bonhoeffer, "Letter to Eberhard Bethge," *Letters and Papers from Prison*, ed. E. Bethge, trans. Reginald Fuller (New York, NY: Macmillan, 1871), 359–361.

18 Karen V. Guth, "Claims on Bonhoeffer: The Misuse of a Theologian," *The Christian Century*. May 13, 2015 (https://www.christiancentury.org/article/2015-05/claims-bonhoeffer).

neighbor, and lowering oneself to hardship is a basic expression of the knowledge of God."[19]

In this manner, the missional community will lower ourselves to hardship for our neighbours. We will be a contrast community in such a way that our time, work, income, and possessions aren't only intended for ourselves, but to be a blessing to the poor and weak. Very practically, amid the global pandemic of 2020–2021, our missional community visited the poor and brought them food. We found ways to bless the least of these when much of the world was in hiding. We took risks for the sake of others in our community.

Psalm 82:3–4 declares, "Defend the cause of the weak and fatherless; maintain the rights of the poor and oppressed. Rescue the weak and needy; deliver them from the hand of the wicked."[20] Deuteronomy 10:18 proclaims, "Ensure that orphans and widows receive justice; show love to the foreigners living among you and give them food and clothing."[21]

In summary, as we connect with our neighbours, the idea is not necessarily to distribute resources, although there may be some exceptions. Good neighbouring isn't about blindly giving handouts to those in poverty, potentially creating dependency and undermining people's dignity in the process. Instead the missional community will engage by *sitting in the midst of poverty*, by being present with those in poverty, ushering peace in the process.

3. Common mission. Missional communities serve a common mission. A common mission is the missional community's unified effort to seek the peace of a particular place or neighbourhood. Over the last several years, our common place has been an

19   Christopher A. Beeley, *Gregory of Nazianzus on the Trinity and the Knowledge of God* (New York, NY: Oxford University Press, 2008), 255.

20   Paraphrased.

21   Paraphrased.

inner-city school in downtown Thorold. This school is the hub of our missional activity.

Practically speaking, I volunteer at the school each week. Two members of our missional community serve on the parent-teacher association. We network with churches and community organizations in the neighbourhood. We organize job fairs in the school's gym in partnership with the YMCA Employment Centre. My wife volunteers in the school store each week. A retired woman in our group reads to students every Wednesday. Our missional community also hosts our neighbourhood dinners in partnership with the school, and we host Bible study dinners in the gym. We help organize school trips and raise money for the betterment of the school. As much as possible, we try to bless the teachers and staff each month with a card or small gift. Overall, our desire is to see the school, families, and staff thrive!

Over the last number of years, we have seen God transform this community in powerful ways through our unified mission. When we began serving in this neighbourhood, we heard horror stories of neighbours getting into brawls when dropping their kids off at school. For many years, the school had a reputation for having very low academic performance. It was common knowledge that one-quarter of the student enrollment changed every spring because families were being evicted, unable to pay rent. They therefore pulled their kids out of the school to move to another city.

In the midst of these challenges, we have sensed God calling us to pray and serve in this neighbourhood with a desire to see these realities changed for the better.

Over the years, it has been beautiful to watch the school flourish in small ways. One of our neighbours noted, "There is a whole new vibe in the school." Another community leader said, "This school has developed a heart for the community."

Other touching examples include seeing families connect at our community dinners and become friends. My wife Karen cultivated a connection between a lonely single mom and a new immigrant mom who was expecting her first child. This single mom took the expectant mom under her wing, offered her support, drove her to appointments, advocated for proper healthcare, and taught her the basics of caring for a newborn.

While we see many stories of transformation—small wins and successes—the cold hard truth is that it may take an entire generation to realize lasting transformation. That is precisely why missional communities need to live with a focused intensity around the common mission: to consistently and patiently work towards the peace of the community, with the long view in mind.

The church in Acts 2 reminds us of the importance of circling our missional wagons around a unified mission. The biblical account tells us that the church consistently prayed together in their community and for their community. They were rooted in their context. They ate together in their neighbourhood. They shared with those who were in need on their streets. They were guests in each other's homes. They sought the peace of their city with great love and unity.

In like manner, missional communities must engage in mission with unity and laser focus. The alternative is to serve in islands or groups of geographical incoherence and disconnect.[22]

As author James C. Fenhagen writes in his book, *Mutual Ministry,*

> The more aware we become of the range of human need that surrounds us, the more overwhelmed we can become to the point that we end up doing nothing.

---

22   Simon Carey Holt, *God Next Door: Spirituality & Mission in the Neighborhood* (Victoria, BC: Acorn Press, 2007), Kindle location 721.

Terence Schilstra

> The secret to the compassionate life is to focus our
> care on a few things that we can do something about.[23]

4. Loving our enemies. Missional communities will love those who hate them. Jesus Christ declared, *"You have heard that it was said, 'Love your neighbor and hate your enemy.' But I tell you, love your enemies and pray for those who persecute you, that you may be children of your Father in heaven"* (Matthew 5:43–45).

Perhaps the most striking dimension of the Franciscan order is the idea of engaging one's enemies. Francis of Assisi notes, "Friend or foe, a thief or a robber, let them receive him kindly."[24] In other words, show love to all, especially those undeserving of it. Yes, that means inviting enemies, criminals, or outcasts into our lives. In a most spectacular way, Francis paints a picture of how missional communities should live:"Therefore all those who unjustly inflict upon us tribulations and anguishes, shame and injuries, sorrow and torments, martyrdom and death, are our friends whom we ought to love much."[25] That is, indeed, a bold statement and example of calling for radical love towards those who hate them most.

Several years ago, our missional community got to know a particular staff member at the community centre where we gather. For some reason, this person developed a deep dislike for our group and consistently made passive-aggressive comments in our direction.

But that all ended after we showed him love. On one specific occasion, our whole missional community went out of our way

23   James C. Fenhagen, *Mutual Ministry: New Vitality for the Local Church* (New York, NY: Seabury Press, 1977), 5.

24   Paschal Robinson, *The Writings of St. Francis of Assisi* (Philadelphia, PA: Dolphin Press, 2008), 25–74.

25   Ibid.

to help him set up, run, and clean up after a community event he was responsible for. What would have required hours and hours of work for this man turned into a simple task when we came together to love and help our neighbour. Since then, we have become wonderful friends, and this man has become an advocate for us in the community. Why? Because he recognized that we exist to add value to our community.

In summary, the world chooses to isolate those it hates. The missional community, however, will choose to practically love those who hate us so that we may fulfill the words of Jesus Christ: *"Love your neighbour as yourself"* (Mark 12:31).

5. Evangelism. Sharing our faith in Jesus is central to missional community life. On a June 13, 2016 podcast, Christian sociologist Joel Thiessen had this to say regarding evangelism:

> Being the good, nice, polite Canadians that we are, we are often afraid to actually tell people about the gospel. We just want to be nice people and hope that others ask why we are a nice person and use that as an opportunity to say "because of Jesus." The problem is, no one has *ever* asked me why I'm so nice.[26]

In essence, Dr. Thiessen is saying that we need to put words to our actions.

There is a high likelihood that our unbelieving Canadian neighbours are just as nice as we are, if not nicer. We must not be disillusioned into believing we are somehow "nicer" than our neighbours. Indeed, our contextual reality is such that Canadians are typically very friendly, kind, and active in their communities.

---

26 Joel Thiessen, "Episode 6, Part Two," NewLeaf Podcast. June 6, 2018 (https://www.newleafnetwork.ca/podcast/new-leaf-project-episode-005-joel-thiessen-part-1), 15:00. Paraphrased.

In fact, studies show that forty-seven percent of Canadians (more than sixteen million people) regularly volunteer or serve in their community in some capacity.[27] Therefore, as Christians, we cannot simply "serve and be kind" while sitting back and waiting for someone to ask about the hope we have within us. We need to share it. Evangelism means sharing the peace and hope we have in Jesus Christ with others with words.

When I worked in the trades a number of years ago, there was one guy I really got along well with at work; we considered each other good friends. I had been especially kind to my friend and had been faithfully praying that God would show him the gift of salvation.

Nevertheless, as the weeks and years passed, I kept thinking, *Man, I've got to clearly share my faith in Jesus with this guy.* He knew I was a Christian and we'd had casual conversations about faith, but I really wanted to share my faith story with him and ask if he had ever considered responding to salvation in Jesus.

In the midst of my waiting for just the right time, and waiting some more, I got a phone call from my supervisor one Friday afternoon on the way home from work. My supervisor told me that there had been a freak accident on one of our job sites and my friend had been suddenly killed. I'd waited so long that I never got the chance to share my faith.

To be clear, whether or not my friend was saved is out of my control. The Bible declares that our salvation and eternal destiny lie solely in the hands of God (Ephesians 2:8, Acts 4:12, Romans 8:28). Yet we do have a certain responsibility to be sharers of the good news even though the results are left up to God.

---

27   "Research About Volunteering in Canada," *Sector Source*. Date of access: January 18, 2021 (http://sectorsource.ca/research-and-impact/volunteering-research).

One man put it this way: "Evangelism is the announcement of good news, irrespective of the results."[28] The goal of evangelism is neither to convert people, nor to win them, nor to bring them to Christ, though this is indeed the first goal of evangelism. Evangelism is simply our call to share the good news with our neighbours.[29]

In 2 Timothy, the Apostle Paul points out that all Christians are called to go and share with our neighbours (and the world) the good news of salvation. Paul writes, *"In the presence of God and Jesus Christ… I give you this charge: preach the word… do the work of an evangelist"* (2 Timothy 4:1–2, 5).

The meaning of the term "preach" in the original Greek is to herald, publicly announce, or proclaim. The word herald is associated with someone in first-century culture who was hired by a king to go through towns announcing important news to the community; after all, there was no CNN or *Thorold News* back then.

In the same way today, we are called to be heralds of the love of Christ and the truth of Scripture to our neighbours. Practically speaking, we are called to speak truth and love into people's lives *"with great patience and careful instruction"* (2 Timothy 4:2) to our neighbours, children, grandchildren, co-workers, friends, and disciple relationships. And we do this in every aspect of life—at work, at play, over meals, and in places we least expect. In all, as people who have been saved from the pit of sin and death, we excitedly share the story of our loving King.

In summary, Malcolm Gladwell tells a story in *The Tipping Point* that stirringly describes the way "news" we share spreads to our neighbours:

---

28 John Stott, "Evangelism," *Christian Mission in the Modern World* (Downers Grove, IL: InterVarsity Press, 1975), 38.

29 Ibid.

On the afternoon of April 18, 1775, a young boy who worked at a livery stable in Boston overheard a British army officer say that there was a plan to attack the town of Lexington, northwest of Boston, to arrest the colonial leaders John Hancock and Samuel Adams, and then march on to the town of Concord to seize the stores of guns and ammunition that some of the local colonial militia had stored there. What happened next has become part of historical legend, a tale told to every American schoolchild. This young boy went to tell this news to a common silversmith by the name of Paul Revere. Revere jumped on a horse and began his "midnight ride" to Lexington. In two hours, he covered thirteen miles. In every town he passed through along the way—Charlestown, Medford, North Cambridge—he knocked on doors and spread the word, telling local colonial leaders of the oncoming British, and telling them to spread the word to others. Church bells started ringing. Drums started beating. The news spread like wildfire as those informed by Paul Revere sent out riders of their own, until alarms were going off throughout the entire region. The word was in Lincoln, Massachusetts, by 1 A.M., in Sudbury by 3, in Andover, forty miles northwest of Boston, by 5. By 9 AM in the morning the warnings had reached as far west as Ashby, near Worcester.

When the British finally began their march toward Lexington on the morning of the nineteenth, their foray into the countryside was met—to their utter astonishment—with organized and fierce resistance.[30]

---

30   Malcolm Gladwell, *The Tipping Point* (New York, NY: Back Bay Books, 2002), 31–33.

The lowly stableboy first heralded certain news to the common silversmith Paul Revere. From his lips, it sounded to thousands of others who shared it with others still, who shared the news across the countryside. Eventually, one by one, the news mobilized an entire region.

I imagine evangelism, sharing the good news of Jesus, works in a similar fashion in our communities. Starting on the lips of a lowly individual, it spreads like wildfire into our neighbourhoods, regions, provinces, and world through the power of the Holy Spirit.

6. Multiplication. The missional community and their leaders must always reproduce and multiply. They will first and foremost multiply their ministry areas by raising up new leaders. Both my wife and I are the byproducts of a wonderful Christian couple who invested in us and taught us to multiply. Similarly, we are investing in the next leaders.

In 2 Timothy 2:2 the Apostle Paul writes to his apprentice, *"And the things you have heard me say in the presence of many witnesses entrust to reliable people who will also be qualified to teach others."* This text is perhaps the clearest example in all of Scripture of how we are called to make disciples and multiply leaders. Simply put, journeymen Christians train apprentices who then become journeymen who train more apprentices.

Furthermore, as the missional community grows or reaches a critical mass, it will send out leaders to start new missional communities in new places of need.

For example, a few years ago, our missional community had a mature Christian couple who sensed God calling them to start a missional community in another neighbourhood. As a group, we prayed over this couple and sent them out with a real excitement to see the gospel take root in a new context. Over time, it has been amazing to see the ways in which this new faith expression has taken root.

In Romans 15:20, the Apostle Paul shares his dream for multiplication, declaring, *"My ambition has always been to preach the Good News where the name of Christ has never been heard…"* (Romans 15:20, NLT) Indeed, Paul had an unending passion to see the gospel expand into new places and spaces.

Another of my favourite examples of multiplication in the history of the church is the life and ministry of Bernard of Clairvaux. This man was truly committed to the growth and multiplication of the gospel and communities of faith. In his early twenties, young Bernard first planted an intentional faith community in France. As its leaders multiplied, the faith community reached capacity. Accordingly, Bernard dispatched waves of leaders to plant new faith communities across the country. By the end of the twelfth century, these faith communities had multiplied into England, Wales, Scotland, Ireland, Spain, Portugal, Italy, and Scandinavia. In his lifetime, Bernard was personally involved in the foundation of no fewer than 163 faith communities. A few years after his death, each of these outposts had multiplied, adding up to 343 communities.

Bernard is one of the most frequently quoted leaders in the church's reformation. John Calvin held Bernard in high regard. Martin Luther called him "the best [Christian] that ever lived, whom I admire beyond all the rest put together."[31] Above all, Bernard was well-regarded for his infectious desire to see the gospel of Christ multiply throughout the world through vibrant communities of faith.

---

31   John F. Thoroton and Susan B. Varenne, eds., *Honey and Salt: Selected Spiritual Writings of Bernard of Clairvaux* (New York, NY: Knopf Doubleday, 2007), xvii–li.

In like manner, missional communities will have an infectious passion for multiplying unique faith expressions throughout their cities and beyond. Practically, I believe the door is open for one missional community to emerge in every community centre and school throughout Canada.

Conclusion

The missional community is called to grow outward by representing the peace of Christ in its community through a lifestyle of repeated actions that grow in intensity. Missional communities adopt consistent habits and practices that directly engage the cultural realities of their community, fostering a deep desire to see not only people's lives transformed by the gospel but their entire neighbourhoods.

Part Two

The Missional Community:
Growing In

A MISSIONAL COMMUNITY IS A GROUP OF PEOPLE WHO actively participate in God's mission to engage God's world, according to his Word. Simply put, God designed Christian community to represent the peace of Jesus in the world, specifically our particular neighbourhoods (Ephesians 3:10).

It is important to note, however, that the missional community can only represent peace when the group evinces a certain level of health and peace. Therefore, this section will seek to cultivate the imagination of missional communities towards the goal of "growing in" together as healthy and functional communities of God.

In the eighteenth century, a wise old Englishman named John Wesley plainly described how intimate faith communities ought to cultivate such health. Healthy faith communities, notes Wesley, "are Christians associating themselves together as a *unified* group to watch over one another in love in order that they might help each other to work out their salvation."[32] Wesley is suggesting that one of the practical ways God cares

---

32   John Wesley, *A Plain Account of the People Called Methodists*. An old church document written by John Wesley to Vincent Perronet on December 25, 1748.

for, guides, and directs his people is within the crucible of Christian community. So the intimate Christian community—the missional community—is designed by God to be a place where Christians exist in unity to support the faith and life of other individual Christians.

In brief, the missional community is an intentional organism created by God where Christians share the gift of life, work out their salvation, look out for one another, and grow together spiritually in the image of Jesus. Practically speaking, missional communities' operative rhythms in this area are as follows.

1. Meeting together. The first and most essential component of Christian community is meeting together. Acts 2:42–46 declares that the central rhythm of the family of God is meeting together *regularly*. The early church didn't meet together for one hour on a Sunday morning; they met *daily* in their homes, in community centres, and in the marketplace.

In the same way, meeting together is central to the life of the missional community. Meeting together, first and foremost, takes *time*. It requires us to carve out a certain amount of time in our schedules to gather with the family of God so our lives might be filled with his peace so we can support each other.

Time is both a depleted and abundant resource in our world. Some people have no extra time and space in their lives; they're running ragged, working extended hours or multiple jobs, getting the kids to programs, etc. Life is stretched thin between responsibilities and to-do lists. This "running ragged" lifestyle is outside God's design and framework for our very existence.[33] Therefore, the living of such a lifestyle ought to give a Christian pause to evaluate whether the frantic life is what God truly desires for us.

On the other hand, there are just as many in our community who have nothing but time; they are crippled with boredom, or by no fault of their own are isolated or disconnected from community.

In each case, missional community members must commit to rhythms in their lives that allow the space to gather together to experience the shalom of Christ and Christian community—peace from the poison of the hurried life, or peace from the monster of isolation. This is a must, because it is essential to our health, our spiritual, physical, emotional, and mental vitality. In other words, Christian community is created by God for us to thrive. Why would we accept anything less?

Practically, the missional community has the amazing opportunity to thrive together by sharing a meal, worshiping,

---

33   "Research bears out the cascading consequences of a rest deficiency. First, lack of rest can compromise health and the quality of work. Heavy workloads and long hours are a significant source of stress in the work place. According to an American Psychological Association survey, more than a third (36%) of workers experience chronic work stress, which can lead to anxiety, insomnia, muscle pain, increased blood pressure, as well as a weakened immune system. This kind of stress can also increase chances of heart disease, diabetes, and depression. Furthermore, exhaustion depletes a person's skill at managing interpersonal relationships. Studies show that when someone is tired he or she misreads other people's social signals. A tired person will project negative motives onto other people, and find it hard to resist lashing out in response. Finally, there are spiritual implications to lack of rest. God created both work and rest, and carelessness in these areas can estrange people from him." See: "Balancing Rhythms of Rest and Work (Overview)," *Theology of Work*. Date of access: January 25, 2021 (https://www.theologyofwork.org/key-topics/rest-and-work-overview).

studying God's Word, praying, engaging in discipleship relationships, and fellowshipping with each other.

2. Enjoy life together. Essential to Christians meeting with other Christians is enjoying life together.[34] We must gather to build connections and friendships through social connections.

Just the other day, a young man here in our city shared with me that the thing he loves to do most is hang out with friends: going bowling, eating fast food, or biking down the canal trail in Thorold. This is a perfect definition of enjoying life.

In the same way, the missional community will be a place of enjoyment. This might take place in our free time, at gatherings, or at social outings. As a missional community, we have attended local hockey games together, or booked group breakfasts at a restaurant on Saturday mornings. We plan a bingo night once a year. Some of us go on hikes together. A group of women meet for coffee every Friday morning, a time that's full of laughter and joy.

Two single women in our missional community hang out and go for coffee each week. Just last week, they saw a movie together. A single dad and I go out for lunch every Friday, and we go for walks and share life together. He invites me to share in his interests, and him in mine. These outings are the highlight of my week!

As people of peace, no one should enjoy life more than us, even in the face of suffering. Therefore, missional community members are encouraged to create space and time to hang out, laugh, and play. This time is essential to deepening our relationships and creating a space where Christians can share the things of life together[35]—sharing our hearts, our joys, struggles, pains, and celebrations.

---

34 John Wesley, *A Plain Account of the People Called Methodists*. An old church document written by John Wesley to Vincent Perronet on December 25, 1748.

35 Ibid.

3. Care together. Missional communities must care for each other in the name of Jesus. John Wesley wrote passionately on how Christian communities might function as places where people love and care for each other. Simply put, he argued that Christians show love and care for other Christians first and foremost by serving the needs of others. Indeed, to love God is to love your Christian neighbour, serving others by carrying each other's burdens. If fellow Christians are in need, help them. If they are sick, visit them. If they are hurting, comfort them.[36] Missional communities must excel in loving and caring for one another.

A few years back, one member of our group expressed that she wasn't doing very well. She felt stressed at work and had fallen short on paying her bills. She was a single mom, divorced, and had two daughters in their early teens.

As she shared her challenges, we asked, "How can we support you?" In response, she immediately broke down, crying. She went on to tell the group that because of workplace issues, she was going to be off work for several weeks. We prayed over her and talked about ways to support her. In the weeks following, being off work created more strain and money problems at home.

Upon hearing more about her situation, I spoke with each person in our missional community to discuss how we could help. We decided to gather some cash and gift cards to give to her. We collected more than a thousand dollars from within the group, gifting that money to her so she could pay the rent and get food for her children. It was amazing to see the way our missional community cared for this woman and helped meet her needs.

Two weeks later, we learned that this single mom had died in a sudden car accident. We were crushed by the news. In the hours following, I called the members of our missional community to inform them about what had happened. Our group fell

---

36   Ibid., 253.

into a state of shock. We met together the next day, a Sunday, to mourn, process, and pray. We discussed how we could support and care for these teenage girls who had just lost their mom.

For our group, her death was a punch to the gut. It seemed impossible to do anything at our gatherings but breathe. All we could do was fall into the arms of God and each other. Over the next days and weeks, our group remained in a malaise. We spent time grieving and supporting each other while exploring options to support these teenage girls.

Overall, this situation, while tragic, tells a beautiful story of how the Spirit of God moves in the heart of Christian community to care for each other's every need.

4. Accountability together. In each area of missional community life, there is space to lovingly hold each other accountable. If someone is absent from a gathering or hasn't been engaging lately, it is the responsibility of the group to gently follow up with that person. This accountability ensures connectivity and health among believers.

Further, special care should be expressed on behalf of the community to ensure that people continue to grow in their faith and spiritual life. Practically speaking, the missional community will cultivate spiritual accountability by creating space in their rhythms to share personal faults, failures, and confession of sins.[37] Indeed, there is a certain humility and vulnerability at play when we as Christians share our weaknesses.

For example, I personally wrestle with the sin of pride and catch myself thinking that I am better than others. God's Word and his Spirit have taught me that this posture is damaging. Therefore, I often say a simple daily prayer for humility and a heart to lower myself to love and serve others.

---

37   Ibid.

Practically, in the context of the missional community, I have a responsibility to share this challenge with other Christians. When I first shared this sin with our group, I discovered that others have the same temptations towards the sin of pride. Consequently, I learned how others deal with and resist this sin. As well, my fellow Christians pray for me in this challenge, asking God to help me gain mastery over it. Furthermore, when I meet with the group they hold me accountable to the sin I have confessed. The group might ask if I've given in to the sin of pride throughout my week. This helps me, because I know I'll be asked about my personal challenge, which then convicts me to resist the temptation, lest I have to confess to the group again that I have continued to be prideful.

Thus, the Christian community works in such a way that Christians hold other Christians together with an accountability filled with gentleness, grace, and love. Otherwise it ceases to be accountability and turns into shaming, which has no place in the community of God.

Again, it is worth restating that accountability is the means by which the Christian community tenderly looks out for each other's best interests. Accountability flows through Christian community in such a way that it always refreshes and encourages Christians as they work out their salvation in Christ together.

5. Pastoral care. Until we receive healing for the wounds of our past, we're going to bleed. We can bandage our bleeding hearts with food, alcohol, drugs, work, money, or sex, but eventually it will all seep through and stain our lives. Yet there is One who can stop the bleeding. His name is Jesus. He provides complete healing. He is our peace.

Pastoral care in a missional framework is rooted in regular people caring for each other in profound ways in the name of Christ. Simply put, through God's Spirit ordinary people have the power to change other people's lives within the safety of the missional community.[38]

Structurally speaking, the high mobility and low overhead of the missional community presents rich opportunities for people-centred care. Therefore, missional communities ought to be prolific in cultivating spiritual and emotional peace in the life of each believer in the group. Practically, there should be space to ask spiritual questions, occasions to share intimate things of life, and opportunities to emotionally connect in deep and profound ways. As a result of people-centred care, each member has the opportunity to find complete emotional and spiritual healing within the life of the group.

Leading Christian counsellor and clinical psychologist Larry Crabb points out in his book *Connecting* that the power of healing is not primarily exhibited in one-on-one therapy, although there is a place for that, but within the Christian community. In fact, Crabb shares that for twenty-five years of his practice, he missed the power of Christ at work within a group of ordinary Christians, which far surpasses the effect of any pastor, counsellor, or therapist.[39] In inspiring vulnerability, Crabb points out that he wasted much of his practice focusing far too much on modern psychology, counselling methods, and his own intellect when attempting to care for people experiencing crisis, loss, brokenness, and hurt.

As an alternative, Crabb declares that first and foremost Christians should see Jesus Christ as the true pastoral care pastor, counsellor, and therapist who has the ultimate power both to prevent and heal emotional, physical, mental, and spiritual maladies.

---

38   Larry Crabb, *Connecting* (Nashville, TN: W Publishing Group, 1997), 31.

39   Ibid.

Further, Crabb laments that Christians tend to seek emotional healing solely in one-on-one counselling, pastoral care, or therapy rather than seeking out God-designed pastoral care and counselling in the care of an intimate Christian community. Thus Crabb proclaims that the real power available to Christians is not found in the isolation of individual counselling, but in discovering the power of Christ *and* his healing hand in the community of God.[40]

As 1 Peter 5:7 declares, *"Cast all your anxieties on [Jesus] because he cares for you."* Galatians 6:2 proclaims, *"Carry each other's burdens, and in this way you will fulfill the law of Christ."*

Therefore, within the missional community, Jesus Christ is the lead pastor of care and primary source of healing. Through Christ, the missional community affirms that the subsequent source of strength is human connection within the group. Practically, healing within the missional community consists of regular people gathering to pray together in the name of Jesus and to vulnerably share their faith challenges and emotions. All the while, space opens within the group as we share how God is progressively at work, bringing healing to our lives and situations.

This healing happens through connection, prayer, and sharing in the context of a Bible study or over weekly meals together. In these times, people become open to sharing their most intimate struggles.

Our missional community has cultivated sharing and intimacy by starting each of our gatherings by going around the circle and allowing each person to share a "rose" and a "thorn"—the rose being a good thing that happened in the week and a thorn being a challenge they experienced. After each person shares, we take some time to pray for the celebrations and struggles the people have shared.

---

40   Ibid, 11.

Bonhoeffer calls this sharing "God's living Word found in the testimony of other Christians,"[41] meaning that through sharing our deepest wounds within the group, we have the opportunity to be cared for, encouraged, and edified by others in the group.

Here's another way to put it: we can find healing for our hearts, minds, and emotions as ordinary people lovingly listen to, pray for, and encourage each other.[42] Indeed, when we do life together, something happens. We proactively and reactively receive the medicine of pastoral care within God's design of Christian community.

Pastoral care in a missional community also requires us to humbly give ourselves to care for physical needs (1 John 3:16). This self-giving care, like the life of Christ, is characterized by action: one must show forth all that is good in deeds towards those within the group.[43]

Practically speaking, each member of the missional community becomes responsible for helping to carry the burdens or needs of individuals within the group, especially in a time of crisis, sickness, death, and loss. All are responsible to visit each other when sick or in the hospital. We make meals for each other in times of pain or need. When there is death in the group, we surround each other with love and care. In all these situations, we pray for each other in the name of Jesus, trusting that God has the power to extend complete healing and peace.

---

41   Dietrich Bonhoeffer, *Life Together and Prayerbook of the Bible* (Minneapolis, MN: Fortress Press, 2004), 32.

42   Crabb, *Connecting*, 31.

43   Benedict of Nursia, *The Rule of St. Benedict*, xxxvi, lxii.

Conclusion

Missional communities find the peace and shalom of Christ in the rhythms of intentional Christian community. As that peace breaks into our lives, it's important to ensure that the missional community doesn't turn completely inward and forget to be agents of peace in their neighbourhoods.

Part Three

The Missional Community: Growing Up

THE APOSTLE PAUL ONCE FAMOUSLY WROTE,

> *And I am convinced that nothing can ever separate us from God's love. Neither death nor life, neither angels nor demons, neither our fears for today nor our worries about tomorrow—not even the powers of hell can separate us from God's love. No power in the sky above or in the earth below—indeed, nothing in all creation will ever be able to separate us from the love of God that is revealed in Christ Jesus our Lord.*
>
> —Romans 8:38–39, NLT

Simply put, God is a God of love who passionately loves his people. In fact, God (Father, Son, and Holy Spirit) invites all humanity into a loving relationship with himself.[44] To know that love is to experience the fullness of peace.

In Proverbs 8:17, the Lord God declares, "*I love those who love me, and those who seek me find me.*" 1 John 4:19, in essence,

---

44   Stephen Seamands, *Ministry in the Image of God: The Trinitarian Shape of Christian Service* (Downers Grove, IL: Intervarsity Press, 2005), 41.

proclaims, "We love God because He poured out His love for us first!"[45]

While God continues to love and care for us, we have a tendency to defect from loving him. In fact, our days are checkered by actions and thoughts that fracture our love relationship and peace with God. This love and peace are fractured because we forget God and develop misplaced affections. This act of misplaced love is what we call sin. St. Augustine put it this way: "The essence of our sin is disordered love."[46]

When I was a teenager, I got the order of love all mixed up—and I still do today.

When I was nineteen years old, I thought the best thing for me would be to live my life my own way. So I moved out of a good Christian home and stopped attending church. I got a solid job and quickly fell in love with money and the stuff it bought, such as a TV, car, clothes, etc. By the time I was twenty, I'd become addicted to work and made a comfortable six-figure salary.[47]

I thought I had everything and I always wanted more. In my pursuit of wealth, I became proud and distant from my family and friends. Worst of all, I distanced myself from God. I didn't need him. I had everything I needed, or so I thought.

Life went on like that for a season, until in my mid-twenties a serious car accident almost cost me my life.

Immediately after the accident, while I was at home recovering in bed, I began reconsidering my priorities. During that time, God worked in my heart.

As I look back on that season, I can see the amazing way in which God pursued me and loved me right where I was, even

---

45   Paraphrased.

46   St. Augustine, Philip Schaff, ed., *The Complete Works of Saint Augustine*.

47   Today my salary is seventy-five percent lower than what it was then, and I live a much fuller life!

though I was far from him. That is when I responded to the decadent freshness of God's salvation and gave myself over to him.

For some reason, during this time I started reading the Bible. Then I began praying and found myself falling into his arms. I asked for forgiveness for my sins, for being so selfish, for focusing my life on things and work instead of on him and others. I received the gift of complete forgiveness from sin and my misplaced affections. In this new season, God brought peace and shalom into my heart. And he gave me new priorities.

The essence of my brokenness was disordered love. While I still make mistakes, I learned that there is a *right order of love* that will ensure that I have genuine fulfilment, freedom, and shalom in my life. The perfect order of love is as follows:

1. Recognizing that our God loves us (1 John 4:19).
2. Responding to God's love because he loves us (1 John 4:19).
3. Developing love for others because God loves them.
4. Loving ourselves because our God loves us as his cherished children.[48]

When our love and affections are in order, we will have real peace with God, with others, and with our community.

How Do Missional Communities Grow Up?

Now that we have a sense of the things that separate us from God, we can begin to talk about how to grow up in our relationship

---

48   I'm not talking about narcissism; I'm talking about being grateful for the way God made us, forgiving ourselves, taking care of our bodies, etc.

with God. This is the most important part of our lives and missional community life. In fact, we cannot "grow out" or "grow in," as outlined in the previous sections of this book, unless we place our relationship with God at the very centre of our lives.

Growing up with God as a Christian and mission community is marked by the following practices.

1. Worship together. Plenty of Christian authors have written *about* Christian spiritual disciplines and worship. Few, however, have written on the actual *practice* of worship, with the exception of St. Benedict and St. Francis. Indeed, these writers offer perhaps the most in-depth practical treatise on growing up in a spiritual relationship with God in the history of the church.

Members of the Benedictine and Franciscan communities literally committed their entire lives to cultivating a love relationship with God. They drew closer to the heart of God by studying the Scriptures together, joining together in prayer, and developing spiritual rhythms of examination, piety, fasting, and silence. These practices weren't vain rituals; rather, they were the fountain of living water from which they drank in the amazing presence of God.

These life-giving practices required them to commit four hours every day to prayer, reading, and memorizing Scripture. These communities were famous for their members' ability to memorize and recite Scripture by heart, particularly memorizing entire Psalms together. The goal of memorization was to cultivate their hearts with the nourishing closeness of God himself in his Word.

At certain times throughout the daylight hours, these communities would sit together in silence to listen to the voice of God. They would gather to sing every day, lifting up their voices to praise him with choruses of "Hallelujah." At night, they roused from their sleep at midnight to recite more Scripture, sing more hymns, and read the lectionary from the Old and New Testaments. Simply put, these rhythms were the means by which individuals and the Christian community deepened their personal love relationship with God.[49]

God invites us as a missional community to commit our lives to deepening our relationship with him through intentional daily practices. Therefore, missional community members ought to commit to daily rhythms of personal Bible study, prayer, and spiritual disciplines. Further, the missional community will gather regularly, at least once a week, to worship God in song, reflect on his Word in the Bible, hear the story of salvation, pray, and take offerings for the poor. Indeed, through these communal gatherings of worship, the peace and shalom of Christ breaks into the heart of the individual and the collective community in a powerful way.

2. Re-enacting the mighty acts of God. Unfortunately, for far too long faith communities have defined worship as a mere gathering on Sunday mornings. Further, we have limited worship to only singing songs and listening to a teacher speak. That is, as noted above, an essential form of worship, but it's very limited in scope. The story of Scripture and the life of Jesus declare that worship is meant to be deeper and wider. The sum of heartfelt Christian worship is more than a slot of time marked on a calendar. Rather, faith communities ought to worship as a lifestyle. Thus, worship is not an event. Worship is the ongoing re-enactment of the mighty acts of God.

The primary form of worship for the missional community is enacting the habits of Jesus in our community to the glory of the King. When Jesus cared for the weak and sick, he glorified the King of heaven. When Jesus broke bread together with his disciples, it was an act of love and worship before God. When he

---

49   Robinson, *The Writings of St. Francis of Assisi*, 48–49.

was a guest at the tables of strangers, he brought fame to his Father's house. When Jesus shared the love of the Father, the angels of heaven rejoiced, praising God.

In these same ways, missional communities will worship the King together by serving others, being hosts and guests at the table of hospitality, caring for neighbourhood needs, being present in the margins, sharing their faith in Christ, and advocating for the weak. Missional communities worship as a lifestyle and re-enactment of the mighty acts of God in their community, thereby giving love, honour, and praise due his name.

One of the original Greek words in the Bible that describes genuine worship is θρησκεία, pronounced *thréskeia*. The foundational meaning of this word is: worship as expressed in common practice.

Specifically, this term suggests that worship is a kind of lifestyle marked by certain actions. For example, James 1:27 notes, "Pure and genuine worship [*thréskeia*] in the sight of God the Father means caring for orphans and widows in their distress."[50] Worship in this case is the common practice of caring for the fatherless and vulnerable, those who may not be able to care for themselves. Accordingly, worship means being present to God as we are present to others. Pure worship means stooping down to serve others in the name of Jesus to glorify our King. In other words, simply being present in the lives of our neighbours is a spiritual act of worship that glorifies God!

Romans 12:1 commands us, *"Offer your bodies as a living sacrifice, holy and pleasing to God—this is your true and proper worship."* Practically speaking, genuine worship is about being present in our communities, exposing ourselves to that which is uncomfortable by welcoming the stranger and meeting the needs of the weak in our context.

---

50   Paraphrased.

God's heart is for the powerless. Therefore it brings praise to him when we serve the least of these. When we collectively demonstrate love to our neighbours, we lift the banner of glory, praise, and worship to God; through these spiritual acts of worship, God brings holistic shalom into our neighbourhoods through us which further glorifies his name.

> *But you, God, see the trouble of the afflicted; you consider their grief and take it in hand.*
>
> —Psalm 10:14

3. The table. We read in 1 Corinthians 1:23–29:

> *The Lord Jesus, on the night he was betrayed, took bread, and when he had given thanks, he broke it and said, "This is my body, which is for you; do this in remembrance of me." In the same way, after supper he took the cup, saying, "This cup is the new covenant in my blood; do this, whenever you drink it, in remembrance of me." For whenever you eat this bread and drink this cup, you proclaim the Lord's death until he comes.*
>
> *So then, whoever eats the bread or drinks the cup of the Lord in an unworthy manner will be guilty of sinning against the body and blood of the Lord. Everyone ought to examine themselves before they eat of the bread and drink from the cup. For those who eat and drink without discerning the body of Christ eat and drink judgment on themselves.*

As a Christian community meets together, they have the opportunity to experience Christ's love, salvation, and forgiveness in the Lord's Supper (breaking bread and sharing in the cup of thanksgiving). As we share in the Lord's Supper, we must understand how it connects Christians to the heart of God and to each other.

At the Lord's Supper, the Christian community experiences the love, forgiveness, and renewal given in Christ Jesus. In the same way that ordinary food and drink nourish our physical bodies, so too do the bread and grape drink at the Lord's Supper surely nourish and refresh our soul for eternal life.[51]

An ancient Christian document entitled the *Heidelberg Catechism* frames the Lord's Supper as a meal by which the Christian is both reminded of and shares in the finished work of Christ. It also states that the Lord's Supper is a place at which one's life is transformed; sharing the bread and the cup is akin to our sharing in both the suffering and divine life of Christ.

So the Lord's Supper is a literal life-changing practice where one's faith is strengthened and the believer's life is propelled forward to live for Christ. It invokes a certain lifestyle, one that is physically and spiritually nourished by the meal, both presently and into eternity.

Further, sharing the Lord's Supper quenches and revives the faith and spirit of the Christian community. It is the supreme promise of love through which the body and blood of Christ was given to bring us complete forgiveness of our sins.

In the same way that Jesus gave us his supreme promise of love and forgiveness, so too do we promise to love and serve each other within the missional community. Therefore, as we experience the love of Christ in the bread and wine, so too must we go from the table showing love and good deeds towards our fellow Christians.

---

51   From "The Lord's Supper" in *Heidelberg Catechism*, a church document published by the Christian Reformed Church in 1987 (Grand Rapids, MI).

Practically speaking, when Jesus shared the Lord's Supper with his disciples, he shared it in the context of a meal, at a table, where his followers reclined with him. In the same way, the Lord's Supper, for missional communities, is a meal shared together at the table, either before or after the meal, as we recline in the presence of Jesus Christ.

4. Prayer. Missional community life and activity is rooted in an ongoing connection with God in prayer. Henri Nouwen declared, "Prayer is the language of Christian community."[52]

I must admit, there have been seasons in the life of our missional community when we didn't have a language of prayer. There were times when prayer was reduced to a few words at the end of our gatherings. It's not that we didn't want to pray; we just didn't take the time to do it. We focused on other things.

We learned from our failures, by the grace of God. There came a moment at a gathering when a lady burst out, "We don't depend enough on prayer." It was a moment that reorientated us towards prayer. In time, we began to pray together more and more, developing a rhythm. As we spent even more time in prayer together, it became a common practice, or language within the group. We became convinced that the health and future of the missional community and our missional activity was solely dependent on the mighty acts of God in response to the prayers of his people!

Practically, we began to grow in our desire to praise, thank, and worship God in our prayer time. We began lifting our celebrations and joys to him. We once again started taking turns praying for each other's needs. We prayed more deeply that God would lead, guide, and direct our path as a group. We

---

52   Henri Nouwen, "Together We Pray to God." Date of access: January 25, 2021 (https://henrinouwen.org/meditation/together-we-pray-to-god).

continue to pray that the peace and shalom of God would break into our community.

As we live on mission, like the church in Acts, we have been learning to pray not for protection, but for boldness:

> *Now, Lord… enable your servants to speak your word with great boldness. Stretch out your hand to heal and performs signs and wonders through the name of your holy servant Jesus. After they prayed, the place where they were meeting was shaken. And they were all filled with the Holy Spirit and spoke the word of God boldly!*
>
> —Acts 4:29–31

In a similar manner, the missional community seeks the boldness of the Spirit in prayer so we may show forth the kingdom of God in our city in word and in deed.

5. Growing together. Every year on our children's birthdays, my wife and I mark on a chart how much they have grown. With excitement, they stand next to the chart to see the measurement.

In the same way, Christian community is where we have the opportunity to mark spiritual growth together.[53] To measure such growth, we can consistently ask questions such as, "Are you learning new things about God? Are you feeling encouraged in your personal faith? How is Jesus shaping your life? What are our rhythms of prayer and Bible reading?" The goal is to have candid and vulnerable conversations about our walk with Christ.

Another creative way we have measured growth together is by giving space at gatherings for each person to speak positively about the gifts and growth we see in a person's life. Practically

---

53   John Wesley, *A Plain Account of the People Called Methodists*. An old church document written by John Wesley to Vincent Perronet on December 25, 1748.

speaking, the goal is to give each person an opportunity to hear a word of encouragement. By doing so, they can hear and see how God has been at work in their lives. Simply put, in this time they are affirmed in their gifts and growth. Each time we have done this, the people have left the room radiating with joy, standing a little taller, and filled with encouragement. As a result, we go from that place with a desire to grow more with Christ and to use our gifts in our neighbourhood.

6. The Word. For the Christian, finding peace and rest can be a daily struggle. A friend once sat across from me at a diner on a cold winter morning. The young man slumped in the bench and declared with frustration, "Every day is a struggle to find peace."

His words captured the truth of life. Even for followers of Jesus, life can be a grind. Yet there is a place to drink the daily water of peace and rest.

I looked into my friend's eyes and asked if he had started his day with prayer and Bible reading, which is something we had discussed several times before.

"Aw…" he sputtered. "I'm too anxious to read or pray." He was dejected. Yet when those words came out, a light came on for him. He thought for a moment, then declared, "Maybe that's just an excuse. Come to think of it, when I start my days with God and read my Bible, they are always better days."

The Word of God is a fountain of peace. The Bible is a letter of peace and love from the King's heart to ours. It is a living book by which God speaks into our hearts and into his world. An essential part of discovering the heart of God and experiencing his peace is discovering the truth of his Word in the Bible. Therefore, Christians and missional communities build and live their lives according to God's Word.

On a warm summer night, I sat on my front porch with a new friend I had met a few months back at a community dinner downtown. This guy had just lost everything. He'd been expelled from a street gang, lost his apartment, and had no money. He'd lost custody of his children… and even lost a tooth due to his addiction to crystal meth. He was now sleeping on a park bench.

As we sat out on the porch, we laughed and told stories as we had done over the last few weeks.

While sipping our cold drinks, we came to a natural pause in the conversation. The sun was poised to duck beneath the horizon.

"Can I read something to you?" I said, breaking the silence.

"Sure," he said in his always-friendly way.

I stepped into the house and came back out with a Bible. I opened it and read from 2 Corinthians 5:17: *"Therefore, if anyone is in Christ, the new creation has come: the old has gone, the new is here!"*

After the last word fell out of my mouth, we sat in silence again as the sun slipped away. I prayed my friend would somehow respond.

He broke the quiet of the moment with these deep and profound words: "I'm going to bed."

He slowly got up and retired to the space my wife had made for him in our basement.

Early the next morning, while having a bowl of cereal back out on the porch, my friend came outside and sat down. He was holding a little Bible that had been beside his bed.

"This might sound really weird," he said. I looked on, hardly listening with sleep in my eyes. "I went to bed last night and read the verses you mentioned." He stumbled for words, then declared: "I think God is making me a new creation."

God saved my friend that night. By his Word.

The Bible is a love letter from the King's heart to ours. God spoke to my friend's heart that night. He showed him that through Jesus, we can find relief from sin and the promise of a new life, even if you're a drug addict with a rap sheet as long as the line-up at a Tim Hortons drive-thru.

My friend was broke. But Jesus, by his Word, made him rich in spirit.

The Bible has the power to transform our lives, and it draws us deeper into the heart of God. It is not merely a book. Rather, the Bible is a divine Word that shines peace into our lives and our world. It serves as both a light into our souls and a map for life. Christopher Wright calls the Bible "a missional phenomenon in itself" that renders to us the divine story of God's mission, redemption, restoration, and shalom.[54]

Therefore, as Christians we must sit under its power in prayer. As missional communities, we must allow the Bible to speak into the soul and heart of the group. After all, it is the primary means by which God shows us how to love him and each other—and it shows us the path to transformation and shalom in our community.

7. Freedom to flourish. The Bible ushers peace into our lives, yet it often does so by acting as a concrete force, like gravity. Gravity has a certain authority moored to reality. In other words, we must accept gravity for what it is.

A man once said, "Gravity does not have authority over my life." Later that day, he walked off a cliff. He felt gravity's authority on the way down and especially at the bottom.

Gravity is simply there. We must not behave as if it were not.

In the same way, the Bible, the King's Word, is simply here with us. We must not behave as if it isn't. It is authoritative over our lives.

When I was a kid, I was in the Cadets. There, we all memorized John 14:15, which says, *"If you love me, keep my commandments."* As an adult and a dad, I have come to understand this

---

54 Wright, *The Mission of God*, 50.

verse a little better. The verse is really just saying, "I want the best for you." When God tells us to keep his commandments, all he's really saying is "I want to see you flourish."

Now, we could say, "The Bible doesn't have authority over our lives"—or we could choose to reject God's commands. But that would be like rejecting what is best for us. Thus, if we choose to live outside the King's commands, we will feel the negative results.

For example, the Bible has a rule that says, "Do not steal." Now, if you steal your neighbour's bike, they're going to be disappointed, at the very least. They might even want it back—which may involve the police coming to your home to seek justice, which may mean punishment for you. In this example, the act of stealing has disrupted the peace of the neighbourhood.

If we reject the authority of the Bible's commands, we disrupt the peace of the city. Therefore, the Bible invites us to live in peace and order. Yes, if we keep God's command and live under His perfect authority, we have amazing freedom to flourish!

In the same way that we can live fruitful lives by respecting gravity and allowing it to become second-nature to us, living by the authority of the Bible offers us the gift of amazing freedom— freedom to live a life of peace both now and beyond. Christopher Wright put it this way: "The authority of the Bible is a direct dimension of reality that constitutes sufficient and meaningful grounds for flourishing."[55]

It is interesting to point out that most of the Bible is not a list of commands. In fact, the Bible is made up mostly of different forms of narrative (story), poetry, prophecy, songs, and letters. While that is true, we must receive the whole Bible, even the parts that do not convey rules, as the story of the King's loving authority over our lives and activities as Christians and a missional community.

---

55   Ibid, 51.

8. People with purpose. The Bible is God's Word to us. As we live by God's Word, we ourselves become God's Word to the world. Yes, we become a Word spoken forth by God. Genesis 2 in essence declares that God spoke each of us into existence to the betterment of our community. In other words, we have been created for a very important purpose—the essence of our createdness is to shine forth the peace and goodness of God.

For the last twenty years, I have specialized in mechanical technology, most recently co-vocationally in concert with ministry. In industry, we reference or describe mechanical systems in two distinct ways: static and dynamic. *Static* is that which is tied down, or stationary; it is something fixed in place like a building, desk, or table. On the other hand, *dynamic* is that which is capable of action and change. Imagine an airplane. Depending on whether it's sitting in a hanger or soaring through the air, it could be either static or dynamic.

When we think about having been created or spoken forth by God into the world, I am sad to say that we often think in static terms. We merely think to ourselves, *Wow! I've been made by God.* That makes us feel special and gives us a sense of purpose, and it's true—God did make us, and we are special—but God speaking us into existence produced something far more significant than static beings. God actively spoke humanity into existence for us to be dynamic, capable of movement, change, and action.

Think of it this way. Living a static life would be like owning an amazing sports car, the car of your dreams, but never driving it. Your friends would come by your apartment and want a ride, but you would tell them that you don't drive the car; it just sits there to look nice. The truth of the matter would be that the sports car might look nice sitting in the parking lot (static), but it wasn't designed to sit; it was created to cruise the streets (dynamic) with the windows down, wind in your hair. It was created to let the engine roar and let the rubber fly. In the same way, we were created by God to roll down Main Street.

We are creatures of action, creatures of monumental purpose. The Scriptures declare that we were made to rule over all living creatures to the glory of God. We were created to positively impact every square inch of our orbit. We were spoken forth by God to be fruitful and nurture growth in our neighbourhood. Ephesians 2:10 declares that we were created in Christ Jesus to do good.

In summary, we are dynamic people of purpose who relentlessly cultivate peace in our context.

Review

By way of review, the last three chapters have outlined the following three rhythms of missional community life:

1. *We grow out together, serving our community.* We are a people of peace called to love and serve our community in the name of Jesus. Specifically, we serve together while cultivating meaningful relationships with our neighbours in a way that is tailored to our contextual realities.
2. *We grow in our relationships with each other.* As a missional community, we strive to holistically love, care, and support each other in the name of Jesus.
3. *Most importantly, we grow up in our relationship with God.* As a community, we long to deepen our relationships with God through a community of spiritual practices.

In conclusion, as we exhibit and practice these rhythms, we will indeed experience *and* represent the peace of God in our neighbourhoods.

Part Four

The Christian Life

THIS PART OF THE BOOK WILL BRIEFLY TOUCH ON THE NATURE of the Christian life. Particularly, it will explore how the Christian is called to live within a missional paradigm.

1. What is a Christian? St. Teresa of Ávila wrote this in the sixteenth century:

> Christ has no body now but yours. No hands, no feet on earth but yours. Yours are the eyes through which he looks compassion on this world. Yours are the feet with which he walks to do good. Yours are the hands through which he blesses all the world... Christ has no body now on earth but yours.[56]

We are the peace of Christ in the world. More specifically, Christians are citizens and representatives of the peace and shalom of the King in our local neighbourhoods.

Christians are God's present peace because we are literally filled with Christ and his Spirit. Galatians 5:16 says that we are

---

56   "Teresa of Ávila Quotes," *Goodreads*. Date of access: January 25, 2021 (https://www.goodreads.com/quotes/66880-christ-has-no-body-now-but-yours-no-hands-no).

"animated and motivated by God's Spirit" (MSG). Cyril of Alexandra wrote, "All of us who have received the Holy Spirit are in a sense merged together with God [Father, Son and Holy Spirit]."[57]

Our situation here on earth would surely be a hopeless mess if the very majesty of God had not descended on us. Yet we haven't been left to such a hopeless state. Rather, we've been filled with the peace of God by virtue of his presence in our body, physically and spiritually.

In the same way that Jesus Christ, being God, entered into the flesh of humanity, so too has the power of God's Holy Spirit entered into our human estate in such a way that his divinity and our human nature are mutually connected and growing together.[58] One of Jesus's disciples, a man named Peter, called this our participation in the divine nature whereby his divine power gives us everything we need for a godly life.[59]

2. Christians follow Jesus. The fact that we are filled with the Spirit of Jesus compels us to a particular state of being and lifestyle: we become people of peace. How do we become people of peace? We follow Jesus who is our peace.

John 6 includes a story in which a huge group of people were following Jesus. It was a loosely organized group truly interested in his life and teaching. Each person had made a real sacrifice to follow him; they had given up their evenings to listen to his teaching and carved time away from their work to see his miracles. Simply put, they really liked Jesus. In fact, John 6 says this group wanted to follow Jesus so desperately that when they found out that Jesus had taken a little boat trip across a lake, they

---

57   Alister E. McGrath, *Christian Theology* (Chichester, UK: John Wiley & Sons Ltd., 2017), 297.

58   John Calvin, *Institutes of the Christian Religion* (Peabody, MA: Hendrickson Publisher, 2008), I.iii.

59   Paraphrased from 2 Peter 1:4.

hustled around the shoreline on foot to catch up with him the next morning.

When they caught up, gasping for air, Jesus invited them to sit and began to teach them.

Close your eyes and imagine that you're sitting on the shoreline with Jesus. Gulls soar quietly overhead. Waves gently lap the beach. A hush moves over the crowd. Jesus looks you in the eye and says these words:

> *I am the bread of life. Whoever comes to me will never go hungry, and whoever believes in me will never be thirsty… And this is the will of him who sent me, that I shall lose none of all those he has given me, but raise them up at the last day.* For my Father's will is that everyone who looks to the Son and believes in him shall have eternal life, and I will raise them up at the last day.
>
> —John 6:35, 39–40 (emphasis added)

Jesus gave the pure gospel to this ragged crowd: the only way to receive salvation and be assured of eternal life is through faith in him. He lovingly said, "*Everyone who looks to the Son and believes in him shall have eternal life.*"

As the crowd heard these words, their hearts were full. They got excited and pressed their feet in the sand towards Jesus, declaring, "We want this salvation and eternal life. We want to follow you, Jesus!"

Except that isn't what happens in the story.

When Jesus declared that following him and placing one's faith in him was the only way to the Father and abundant life, the people were shocked. They started to grumble and fume.

John 6:60 tells us, "*On hearing [these words], many of his disciples said, 'This is a hard teaching. Who can accept it?'*" Aware that

51

this gang of followers were grumbling, Jesus said to them, "*Does this offend you? ... This is why I told you that no one can come to me unless the Father has enabled them*" (John 6:61, 65).

With love, Jesus in essence said, "Follow me. Put your life in my hands. I am the way of life. I am the way to the Father." Yet when he said this, his followers threw up their hands and split. John 6:66 says, "*From this time many of his disciples turned back and no longer followed him.*" This huge group of people had sacrificed so much to follow Jesus, but now they just said "Forget it" and took off.

Why does this happen? The fuming crowd walked away because they wanted to hold onto their life *and* have eternal life. They wanted to keep their sin *and* receive God's forgiveness. They wanted a relationship with God *without* his Son. They were willing to make a small sacrifice, but not a complete sacrifice. They wanted salvation without faith.

In short, they wanted the cheap Jesus. They only wanted to follow Jesus half-heartedly. Oh, sure, they had made sacrifices, but they didn't want to bet their entire lives on Jesus. They could run from here to there with Jesus and handle getting tired out as they followed him, but they couldn't handle actually placing their lives in his hands. That would require taking the risk of faith.

When the crowd took off and the dust settled, Jesus turned around and to his surprise there remained only a small huddle of people staring at him deer-eyed. Jesus said to them, "Aren't you going to take off too?"

A guy by the name of Peter, one of Jesus's disciples, piped up: "*Lord, to whom shall we go? You have the words of eternal life. We have come to believe and to know that you are the Holy One of God*" (John 6:68). Peter laid everything on the line. He said, "I'm all in. I put my faith in you alone. I follow you!"

Peter made a clear declaration of what it means to be a Christian: *"We have come to believe and know that you are the Holy One of God."*

If you sense God inviting you to make this declaration, take time to pray these words: "God, show me how I can come to believe and know Jesus!"

John Piper once wrote, "Lord, wherever we look for another Lord, another way, another friend, another philosophy, another view of God, another salvation, another meaning, they all come up short. We can't walk away. You have the words of life."[60]

In his book *The Spirit of the Disciplines*, Dallas Willard gives us a helpful and practical illustration of what it looks like to follow Jesus.

Imagine a group of teenagers who are in love with their favourite professional baseball players and imitate their every move. This group of teens goes to great lengths to look just like the player they love: they buy the same shoes and wear their hats. When the teens play a baseball game, they wiggle the bat and slide into second base, just like their Major League Baseball heroes.

However, while the teens *act* like their favourite players, they do not in any way *perform* like them. The fact is that the teens merely imitate their heroes, but they don't want to do any of the hard work, sacrifice, and practice it takes to be great players.[61]

In the same way, as we follow Jesus we are not merely to act like Jesus. We don't put on clothes to look like followers of Jesus. We don't just imitate his life. Instead, through the consistent

---

60   John Piper, "You Have the Words of Eternal Life," *Desiring God*. December 20, 2009 (https://www.desiringgod.org/messages/you-have-the-words-of-eternal-life).

61   Dallas Willard, *The Spirit of the Disciples* (New York, NY: Harper Collins, 1991), 3–5.

daily practice of submitting to the Spirit of God which lives in us, we are daily shaped by God into the *exact image* of Jesus.

Following Jesus is not an act or performance. It is an act of faith and submission. And it does not start with perfection. It starts right where we are, by taking one small step of obedience, one step towards a lifestyle of Christlikeness that grows in intensity throughout our lives.

Recently, a young man in our community came to Christ. He is a single dad, twenty-three years old. While learning to follow Jesus, he wrote these beautiful words:

> Hi, my name is Nick. I have struggled with loss, sorrow, grief, anxiety, and anger. A year or so ago, my fiancée and I split up. I became very depressed and started having suicidal thoughts. During this time, I started attending community dinners hosted by The Table Missional Community. While there, I met many great people. One of those people really invested in me. He and I would go on to become great friends. We would go for walks, breakfast, or lunch each week. During those times together, we talked about God and his love. One morning we prayed together and I asked Jesus Christ to be my saviour.
>
> After my experience with coming to Christ and joining a missional community, I started to show up at their gatherings regularly. The more I went, the more free and peaceful I felt. I felt more connected with God and was feeling him freeing me from my sins. I also started praying to God more. Something I never expected to do. I pray for a better future for myself and my two-year-old son. I pray that I will grow to trust in the Lord more every day. Philippians 4:6 says, *"Don't*

worry about anything; instead, pray about everything. Tell God what you need, and thank him for all he has done." [NLT] God, thank you for all you have done in my life!

In this letter, Nick beautifully describes what it means to follow Jesus, especially when he writes, "I pray that I will grow to trust in the Lord more everyday." Nick is on a journey, a journey marked by small steps of trust.

3. What are the marks of the Christian life? In the Disney movie *Beauty and the Beast*, the character Lumière, a candlestick, has a line that defines his life when he proclaims, "Life is so unnerving for the servant who is not serving!"[62]

This motto defines the Christian life: servanthood. As agents of peace who are filled with the incarnation of the King, we set nothing before us but the necessities and the advantage of others. Martin Luther put it this way: "The Christian is the most dutiful servant of all, and subject to everyone."[63]

God calls the Christian to many virtues, but the greatest is love, and the greatest expression of love is suffering with and for others.[64] Sacrificing ourselves for our neighbours, caring for the poor, and lowering ourselves to hardship is the primary expression of the knowledge of God.[65]

We are servants because Jesus Christ our King was a servant who served others both in life and in death. He cared for

62 *Beauty and the Beast*, directed by Gary Trousdale and Kirk Wise (Los Angeles, CA: Walt Disney Pictures, 1991).

63 Martin Luther, *Concerning Christian Liberty* (New York, NY: P.F Collier & Son, 1910), 336–378.

64 Brian J. Matz, *Re-Reading Gregory of Nazianzus: Essays on History, Theology, and Culture* (Washington, DC: The Catholic University of America Press. 2012), 58.

65 Beeley, *Gregory of Nazianzus on the Trinity and the Knowledge of God*, 255.

Terence Schilstra

those who were hurting and spent time with the outcasts. He washed his disciples' feet. Most of all, Jesus Christ served in death by giving his life for us.[66] Having nothing before himself but the necessity and advantage of others, Jesus Christ is the model and form of servanthood.

As Jesus's followers, we are commanded to serve our neighbours. Martin Luther declares, "Because Jesus Christ gave himself for me, I will, therefore, give myself as a sort of Christ to my neighbour."[67] What he was saying is that Jesus Christ committed himself to serving us, so we commit ourselves to serving our family, neighbours, and friends.

Practically speaking, what does this look like? The Bible declares, *"Stoop down and reach out to those who are oppressed. Share their burdens, and so complete Christ's law. If you think you are too good for that, you are badly deceived"* (Galatians 6:2, MSG). As Jesus served us in our lowly state, so should we also focus on serving those who are most in need: the weak, the minorities, and the powerless.

Suffice it to say, we do not serve people who are just like us. We do not seek to love only people of peace. Rather, as the Bible declares, "If you are kind only to your friends, how are you different from anyone else? Even pagans do that." We are called to sacrificially love not just our friends, or people of peace, but to serve those in the margins and even our enemies.

Jesus declares, "I say to you, love your enemies! Pray for those who persecute you! In that way, you will be acting as true children of the King of heaven and earth" (Matthew 5:44–45).[68] According to Jesus's command, the heart of servanthood and missional engagement is being present among those who are least

---

66   Luther, *Concerning Christian Liberty*, 336–378.

67   Ibid.

68   Paraphrased from Matthew 5:44–45.

like us. By serving in this way, we represent the peace and shalom of God in the world.

4. The process of servanthood. As we grow as followers of Jesus, there is a traditional four-step process to help guide us towards servant activity as agents of peace:

1. We receive the gift of faith and salvation in Jesus Christ.[69]
2. Through the gift of faith in Jesus, we are raised up by God above ourselves to be children of the King. Imagine, a King knighting us into royalty!
3. As children of the King, we are called to sink below ourselves to serve others in his kingdom.[70] [71]
4. Through our acts of servanthood, the King brings about peace in our neighbourhoods *through us* (not ourselves).

It is important to note that we cannot earn the gift of faith, salvation, or heaven through a life of servanthood. Instead we must know that serving others is the work of Jesus at work in us, which is his gift to others in order that they might know his love.

---

69 Faith is solely a gift from the Holy Spirit and we can ask to receive that gift. Ephesians 2:8 declares, *"For it is by grace you have been saved, through faith—and this is not from yourselves, it is the gift of God"* (Ephesians 2:8). So faith is dispensed by our loving Father and King to all those who ask for it. By asking, faith takes root in our being and we become the presence of Christ in the world. Here's another way to put it: we receive and embody the unspeakable love, salvation, and mercy of God. Through the power of God, we become his peace in the world. As his children, we are agents of restoration and wholeness.

70 Luther, *Concerning Christian Liberty*, 336–378.

71 Heino O. Kadai, "Luther's Theology of the Cross." *Concordia Theological Quarterly*, July 1999. Quoting Martin Luther.

Servanthood is Jesus's way of working through us to show others his love and peace. Therefore, Christian servant activity is the work of Jesus, not us. As Christians we must set aside our reliance on works and set a course to strengthen our faith in Christ alone, which then produces servanthood in the world.[72] In this way, the peace of Jesus breaks into our world.

5. Servants at baptism. In a sense, our servanthood begins at baptism.[73] Baptism is our initiation into a life of serving others, embracing weakness, and welcoming suffering that will change us and by extension others.

In 2017, there was a man and woman in our neighbourhood who attended our community dinners. After both had seen and heard the love of Jesus through members of our missional family, they received the gift of salvation in Christ.

Afterward, they read in their Bibles that Jesus commanded his followers to be baptized. Accordingly, they asked to be baptized. At their baptism, four things happened in their lives, the same four things that have happened to millions of people who have been baptized throughout the history of the church.

First, when they were baptized they admitted with a lowly heart their sin and brokenness within the love of the Christian community, declaring that only Jesus could rescue them from their sins. To all those who are saved, the Bible says, *"Repent and be baptized, every one of you, in the name of Jesus Christ for the forgiveness of your sins"* (Acts 2:38).

Second, baptism was an opportunity for them to publicly declare that they had placed their faith in Jesus Christ and committed to following him as servants with their whole lives, by the grace of God.

---

72 Luther, *Concerning Christian Liberty*, 336–378.
73 Whether we're baptized as a child or adult.

Third, baptism by water was a physical sign that they had received and submitted to the Holy Spirit's work in their lives, in obedience to God's Word. Thus, baptism is an outward act signifying the inward reality that our hearts have been illuminated by the physical presence of the Holy Spirit so we can follow Christ, to the glory of our Father.

Fourth, at baptism, they submitted themselves to the love of the missional community, and the missional community mutually submitted to them. As an extension of that commitment, they joined the missional community in its commitment to serve its neighbours together in the name of Christ.[74]

74   For further reading, I would recommend "The Lord Prayer" in *Heidelberg Catechism*, a church document published by the Christian Reformed Church in 1987 (Grand Rapids, MI).

Part Five

Missional Leadership

THE MISSIONAL LEADER IN THE TWENTY-FIRST CENTURY IS called to know the highest ethic of God's character: love. God's amazing love reverberates throughout history and the Bible, the apex of which is Jesus Christ's loving sacrifice on the cross.

To miss God's love is to overlook his nature. The Bible declares, "*The Lord, the Lord, the compassionate and gracious God, slow to anger, abounding in love and faithfulness, maintaining love to thousands, and forgiving wickedness, rebellion and sin*" (Exodus 34:6–7). Psalm 136 proclaims that the steadfast love of God endures forever. Therefore, the missional community leader is called to know such love and live in the world with that knowledge.[75]

1. Broken love. The Christian leader above all is a trailblazing ambassador for making God's love known in the world. In today's post-modern, post-Christendom culture, showing forth God's love in a given context will require an amazing amount of creativity and ingenuity.

The good news is that God has wired humanity to be inherently innovative. Moreover, as church planter and author Alan Hirsch suggests, this innovative DNA runs especially deep among

---

75   H.J.M. Nouwen, *In the Name of Jesus* (Spring Valley, NY: Crossroad Publishing ,1989), 41.

Terence Schilstra

leaders.[76] The bad news is that Christian leaders are especially good at using their innovative minds to invent their own ministry methods rather than following the methods of God. In particular, if unchecked, they innovatively pursue their own desires.

In 2 Samuel 12, we see an example of this depraved innovative pursuit in the life of the great leader David.

One day the prophet Nathan came to David with a scathing account in which an incredibly wealthy and powerful man stole and killed a poor man's only possession, a helpless young lamb. Upon hearing this report, David fumed with rage, vowing as leader and king to rain punishment on the wealthy man for his treatment of the unfortunate individual, not to mention the murder of the vulnerable lamb.

When David finished his self-righteous diatribe, Nathan looked him square in the eyes and said, "David, you are the leader in the story!" He then implicated David for playing the role of the powerful leader who innovatively erases another life to get what he wants: *You struck down Uriah the Hittite with the sword and took his wife [Bathsheba] to be your own*" (2 Samuel 12:9).

Like the modern-day leader, David was innovative. If you know the story of David and Bathsheba, you're aware of the considerable lengths David went to in order to realize his own desires. By doing so, this epic leader, a man after God's own heart, concocted a love other than God's. He applied his enterprising leadership abilities in such a way that he purposely defied God's supreme ethic of love as self-sacrifice for the sake of self-satisfaction, the complete antithesis of God's supreme ethic.

Accordingly, missional leaders must be attentive to the depravity of our entrepreneurial hearts.

---

76   Alan Hirsch, "The Spirit of Innovation: Creating New Futures for the Jesus Movement," *The Permanent Revolution* (San Francisco, CA: Jossey-Bass, 2012), 183–204.

62

2. Grace-filled love. Thankfully, David's story doesn't end there. When he realized the deceptive capabilities of his heart, he fell broken before God, crying out, "*I have sinned against the Lord*" (2 Samuel 12:13).

In like manner, the missional leader of today must have a profound sense of our iniquitous propensities and be willing to admit those faults. As we recognize our weakness and confess our sins, we find the enormity of God's love. Author Steven J. Cole put it this way: "God must break us of our self-dependence so that He can bless us as we cling to Him in our brokenness."[77]

As missional leaders, we must present our fractured self to him daily, because that's where we find our strength and blessing—in his grace. Tim Keller, a church planter in New York, has put it this way: "What [we] need most in a leader is someone who has been broken by the knowledge of his or her sins and even greater knowledge of Jesus' costly grace." So we must lead with a repentant heart, coupled with the assurance that God's great ethic of love covers our innovative faults.

3. Consequences. Of course we have God's grace, forgiveness, and love, but we must also be profoundly aware that even in the arena of grace, there are consequences for our actions. As was the case with King David, if we concoct our own existential vision of "love," we will without question disrupt peace in our community in the process.

On this matter, Bonhoeffer notes, "Every idealized image that we impose on our community will become a hindrance to genuine community."[78] That is, when we as leaders use our po-

---

77   Steven J. Cole, "Broken, but Blessed," *Bible.org*. Date of access: January 18, 2021 (https://bible.org/seriespage/lesson-59-broken-blessed-genesis-3222-32).

78   Bonhoeffer, *Life Together and Prayerbook of the Bible*, 31.

sition of leadership to exact our own "loving" compulsions, we inflict irreversible damage on the group.

There is no doubt that David's secret sins destroyed Uriah's family. Further, David brought calamity upon his home.

Yes, God's grace abounds in our faults, but we must realize that our ethical and moral decisions are social events. That is, if we as leaders give in to our depraved impulses, there is guaranteed to be negative consequences on society.

4. Isolation. There were also times when King David attempted to lead in isolation, especially when sewing discord. When Nathan called out David's sin, David was oblivious to the depravity of his actions.

Consequently, the missional leader in the twenty-first century must not lead without the regular insights of a Nathan in their life. Yes, it is the Holy Spirit who convicts us of sin, but we must not exclude the possibility that God has placed others in our lives to speak candidly on the Spirit's behalf.

Therefore, it is essential for Christian leaders to have at least one person holding them accountable in the arena of leadership. This might be a godly friendship, like the one between David and Jonathan, or a spiritual mentor relationship such as the one between David and Nathan.

Personally, my Nathan is a long-time friend who has the guts to shoot from the hip. This honesty comes from a deep level of trust which has formed over years of messy relationships.

These bonds must, of course, consist of vulnerability and humility, where deep personal matters are shared and called forth. This candour should also require two people to confess their sins to each other.

The church is full of prideful leaders who dare not show their faults or sins. The missional leader will be different. We will be marked by our vulnerability and humility.

Bonhoeffer declares, "In another Christian's presence I am permitted to be the sinner that I am, for there alone in all the world the truth and mercy of Jesus Christ rule."[79] Accordingly, let Christ's grace abound in mutually accountable relationships where we share the depths of our hearts. To lead any other way is to commit leadership suicide.

5. Chasing God's heart. When it comes to knowing the heart of God and living in the world with that knowledge, the psalmist may be one of the most stunning exemplars. After all, God himself called David *"a man after his own heart"* (1 Samuel 13:14). This confirms the life and heart of David, standing as an extraordinary signpost for Christian leaders to exclaim, "I too want to be a leader after God's own heart. I will faithfully do everything he wants me to do."

6. Worship. David pursued God's heart. Though at times he slipped up, the overwhelming majority of David's story proclaims his loving devotion to God. The first and most striking example of this is David's desire and ability to worship. Many of David's psalms express heartfelt love and adoration towards God.

Above all, David recognized that following God's heart meant exalting his name. In the same way, Christian leaders in the twenty-first century must be devoted to calling to the Lord *"who is worthy of praise"* (Psalm 18:3), especially in the midst of endless cultural white noise.

As a leader, take time to give God the bandwidth he deserves in personal expressions of adoration,[80] praise, prayer, Scripture reflection, music, and song.[81]

---

79   Ibid., 32.

80   Many psalms are intimate and personal worship expressions just between David and God.

81   If it has been a while since you praised God, take the time to worship him now!

Lastly, in authentic worship, we come to realize our helplessness as leaders. Jeremiah declared, "Our lives are not our own; it is not for us to direct our steps."[82] To lead is to submit to the Father, worship him alone, and follow in his steps. Jesus put it this way: *"I have come down from heaven not to do my will but to do the will of him who sent me"* (John 6:38). Accordingly, Christian leaders are called to follow God's heart, by giving up their will and submitting to his purposes.

7. Vision. Today, many are writing and speaking about the need for Christian leaders in the twenty-first century to be visionaries, innovators, and entrepreneurs. Yes, such giftings will need to be vigorously and faithfully applied as we serve in God's kingdom. However, these gifts must be exercised faithfully.

In particular, we must understand as entrepreneurs that we must not pursue *our own* entrepreneurial vision. Rather, we must participate in God's own entrepreneurial efforts. In order to do this, we must first and foremost seek God in prayer along with the community of God. That is, missional leaders must realize that to be visionaries, innovative or entrepreneurial, the first goal is to seek God's voice, remembering that his voice always sounds like Scripture. Then, with God's direction, we seek ways to creatively apply God's purposes within our particular context.

It is key to apply God-given vision in our given context. Practically applying vision will always come with a set of core practices. In other words, we can write all the flowery vision statements we want, but if we don't outline and employ core practices that correspond with the vision, the vision is just fluff.

The American energy corporation Enron is said to have been among the most vision-driven corporations of its time. It had wonderful vision statements declaring the company's drive towards innovation and excellence. These flowery propositions

---

82   Paraphrased from Jeremiah 10:23.

hung on their office walls, websites, ads, and billboards. Of course, Enron turned out to be one of the most corrupt corporations of the twentieth century. They lived by the facade of vision statements, not by core practices of actual innovation and excellence.

The lesson for us as missional leaders is this: be leaders of missional practice. In other words, actions speak louder than words.

8. Proving faithful. In a striking instance in the life of King David, God's purposes required nothing more of him than to prove faithful to what he had been asked to do.

The crucial moment of faithfulness occurred when God commissioned David to prepare for the future temple's structure and human resources. In 2 Samuel 7, God revealed a spectacular vision for what would become his holy Tent of Meeting, the central structure where the community would worship the Lord Most High. As God revealed the plan, he made it abundantly clear that David was not to build the temple. Instead, this charge was given later to his son, Solomon.

Although God prevented David from taking part in the actual temple's construction, he was indeed called to contribute by ensuring that those who built the temple had the resources and tools for success. Accordingly, David gathered a team to cultivate their competencies to serve as future leaders.

David didn't lay the cornerstones for the temple, but he trained leaders for the task. Under David's direction, this team shaped the chief cornerstones for the foundation, importing precious resources and fashioning tools to equip the workers.

In this part of the temple construction story, a key leadership imperative emerges: like David, we as leaders must set up our team for future success. The essential component of a team executing a project, let alone starting it, is to have the right plan, tools, and supplies to perform the task ahead.

In the business world, I have grown to like the saying that tells us, "No plan, no parts. No parts, no project. No project, no progress." Missional leaders can apply this principle also. As leaders, like David, we are responsible for ensuring that our team has the right instruction, the necessary tools, and the resources to step out into God's mission. This means practically preparing people with the parts and pieces required to enact God's plan.

For example, if we have a team leader whose role is to set up and take down chairs and tables for our gatherings, then we need to help that leader understand the responsibilities associated with the task—such as the start time, how many chairs and tables are needed, and where they should be set up. If we don't specify simple tasks, tools, resources, and expectations, our team will most likely fail.

9. The why factor. Another key principle David employed is something we might call the *why factor*. In other words, why are we doing what we are doing? For David, he explained the why: *"to [seek] the Lord your God"* (1 Chronicles 22:19).

Similarly, we are called to lead in such a way that people understand the reason they are making disciples, setting up chairs, making food, etc. It is to glorify God. Furthermore, we help our team see God in our tasks, encouraging them to see God at work in the day-to-day stuff of life.

As David set the supplies in place for his team to flourish, he addressed his future leaders: *"Now devote your heart and soul to seeking the Lord your God. Begin to build the sanctuary of the Lord God"* (1 Chronicles 22:19). Notice that David instructed his leaders not just on matters of the task, but on the why factor.

10. Leadership delegation. 1 Chronicles 23–28 highlights perhaps the largest delegation of leaders recorded in the Bible. King David assembled the leaders of Israel to establish a national leadership structure (1 Chronicles 23:2). At the centre of this summit was David's appointment of twenty-four thousand people to work as God's leaders in the temple and serve the community and nation's spiritual needs.[83] In this case, David handpicked the core leadership from an aggregate of more than thirty-eight thousand people (1 Chronicles 23:2).

He delegated to this leadership team a variety of responsibilities within the new temple, including the role of temple priests, musicians, gatekeepers, treasures, and lay officials. David dutifully crafted crystal-clear lists of leaders and their duties, all of which, by the way, were precisely recorded for us to read today (1 Chronicles 25–27).

In so doing, David, perhaps unintentionally, modelled one of the most essential tasks for the modern-day leader—namely, to call people into meaningful positions of leadership.

Further, each leader was given an impeccably clear job description. For instance, David assigned to the sons of Asaph, Heman, and Jeduthun the clearly defined task of temple worship leadership: playing lyres, harps, and cymbals. He then organized these leaders into twenty-four leadership teams, with a duty roster of responsibilities being given to each group along with a schedule to serve for two weeks of each year, based on a lunar calendar of forty-eight weeks. Thus, every team knew their job title, service schedule, and job description.

Now we move to the modern-day leader of missional community. If an archaeologist unearths our missional activities two centuries from now, will they know precisely who was responsible for each task, along with a coherent description for each responsibility? If not, it's time to get to work.

---

83   The Hebrew text notes that thousands of "groups" or "units" of leaders were assembled, most likely an indeterminate number of people numbering in the tens of thousands.

11. Humility. As David executed the preparation process for the temple's construction and a working team, he exhibited stunning humility, while also showing certainty that God had ordained him as leader. In a foundational sense, David was acutely aware that God had called him to be a leader, declaring, "The Lord God of Israel chose me to be a leader!"[84] The epic king rested in the purpose and knowledge that God had called him to lead.

In the same way, modern leaders must have a profound and confident assurance of the task to which they are called. This confidence may be all we have to spur us on to purpose-filled leadership when we're in deep valleys. Therefore, be self-assured in what God has led you to do!

Yet in this call we must find humility. Indeed, the God of the universe has tapped us on the shoulder, a humbling responsibility which deserves a humble response.

David also knew *why* he was a leader: to call people to know God and serve him with a whole heart and willing mind. David was consistent in reminding his family, leadership team, and nation to chase after the heart of God. As leaders, we are not asking people to follow us; we are pointing to God, saying, "Follow him." The Christian leader doesn't seek upward mobility, such as personal fame, but rather downward mobility, denying oneself and humbly pointing to God.[85]

12. Prayer. Near the end of David's life, in a stunning conclusion recorded in 1 Chronicles 29, he prayed over his family, leaders, and nation. David's prayer thesis, if you will, was asking God to direct the heart of his people. David called the nation to know the highest ethic of God: his love for them. Moreover, he prayed that they would live in the world with that knowledge, wholeheartedly (1 Chronicles 29:19).

---

84   Paraphrased from 1 Chronicles 28:4.

85   Nouwen, *In the Name of Jesus*, 91.

In the same way, missional leaders must consistently lift their team up before God in prayer.

Part Six

Missional
Community Structures

THE GOAL OF THIS SECTION IS TO BOTH DECONSTRUCT
unhealthy structures of authority in Christian community and
subsequently reconstruct a biblical model which ought to define
the structure of the missional community. Ultimately, the view is
to inspire all Christians to embrace essential roles within the missional community and empower them to missional engagement.

The foundational statement in this section is this: every
Christian has a role and function within the missional community. There are no benchwarmers. Furthermore, the aim of this
section is to implore ordained leaders to share responsibilities
and the task of mission. It was Hendrick Kraemer who declared,
"At present we are called to rise above the historical imprison-
ment of hierarchical ecclesiological limitations and rethink the
nature, calling and implementation of the church engagement
quite afresh."[86]

1. Deconstructing roles. The missional community is in
default when it defines itself in institutional terms. Central to
modern-day ecclesiology is an avowed principle of government
and power. This principle subscribes to the false idea that the

---

86   Hendrik Kraemer, *A Theology of the Laity* (Vancouver, BC: Regent Col-
       lege Publishing, 1958), 83.

motive force of our faith communities is the structures and government of the organism itself. These structures include hierarchies within meetings, groups, gatherings, and worship. Leadership roles are indeed essential.

However, unhealthy hierarchies emerge when pastors, staff, team leaders, elders, or deacons assume exclusive roles in the church, thereby disenfranchising other missional community members. We hear examples of such disenfranchisement when people say, "I'm not a deacon, so I don't visit the sick," "I'm not a pastor, so I don't teach," or the implied principle of "You're not a leader, so your voice doesn't matter." Such structures both embolden leaders towards the sin of power and relegate missional community members to passive participation.[87]

2. Reconstructing roles. The motive force of the missional community is not the institutional and governmental structures. Rather, faith communities are to be a movement, an organic creature proceeding from the will of God (Ephesians 2).

The following missional community structure applies:

1. Jesus Christ is the Head of the missional community.
2. The missional community is the equal body of Jesus Christ.

As such, the movement of the group is as a unified whole subordinate to the Head, which is Christ. Each and every Christian's role, as part of God's body, is as an equal and active participant in the life and mission of the missional community.

There are, of course, still specific positions of leadership within the missional community. Indeed, leadership is essential to the well-being and spiritual growth of Christian community.

---

87 Ibid., 81.

In the same way that Christ and the apostles named leaders in the church, the missional community will place the care of Christians in the group under the direction of mature Christian leaders (Acts 14:23, Titus 1).[88]

Practically speaking, these spiritual leaders must be mature Christians who have been a Christian for more than five years. As leaders, they must be men and women who are committed to following Christ and live according to Scripture.

The responsibility of the missional leader is to serve the missional family in the name of Christ: to nurture the group as they grow up in their relationship with God, to encourage them to grow in relationship with each other, and to grow out to serve their community.

St. Francis defines leadership this way: "To be a leader is to serve the other."[89] The leader is not one who lords it over the group, in search of more power, but one who considers themself nothing in humble service to those in the Christian community.

So leadership responsibilities are not to be taken lightly. The leader will strengthen the souls of the disciples, encouraging them to continue in their faith and push them through many challenges (Acts 14:22).

While there are specific roles of leadership, these roles are for the purposes of encouraging those within the missional community. Throughout the history of the church are impressive instances of "regular" Christians who act significantly to transform the church and culture.

We see this beginning in the infant church in Acts, through the Patristic Era, from the Middle Ages to the Reformation, and

---

88   John Wesley, *A Plain Account of the People Called Methodists*. An old church document written by John Wesley to Vincent Perronet on December 25, 1748.

89   St. Francis of Assisi, *First Rule of the Friars Minor*, lvii.

from the Great Awakening in America to the modern missional church movement in the 1950s. In each of these eras, many "regular" Christians have made a lasting impact on the church and culture, the likes of whom include Cyprian of Carthage, Francis of Assisi, John Calvin, and John Bunyan, right on down the line to the Wesleyan and Moody charismatic movement.[90]

Indeed, as this was true throughout the history of the church, so too will the future health of the missional church be defined by each Christian playing an essential role as an ambassador of peace in the community.

90   Kraemer, *A Theology of the Laity*, 48.

Community Profile[91]

This section of the book will examine the social demographics present in downtown Thorold and theologically reflect on the community. This examination of downtown Thorold has a view towards comprehending the past and present realities of Thorold in order for our missional community to meaningfully engage the downtown neighbourhood moving forward, culminating in a set of theological responses by which the missional community might participate in the area's transformation. It is intended to be an example of how to go about understanding one's particular context.

The history of Thorold. The earliest records concerning the inhabitants of the Thorold region come from the writings of Jesuit missionaries in 1626, who documented the peaceful Indigenous tribes that dwelled in this part of the Niagara Peninsula.

Nearly two centuries after the Jesuits arrived, Europeans began to settle in the region. By 1817, the township of Thorold was established, boasting a population of 830 people. As Thorold grew, it became known as one of the most economically

---

91   Much of the information about Thorold in this profile is drawn from unpublished booklets which were found at the Thorold Public Library. The titles of the booklets are *Thorold: Its Past and Present*, *Town of Thorold: 1850 to 1950*, and *Thorold's Centennial Book*.

prosperous communities in the Niagara Region, perpetuated by abundant resources and developing trade routes.

Consequently, the population in the area ballooned. By 1841, Thorold housed a population of 3,695 people. In time, it became a key trading hub situated on the new Welland canal route. The canal connected Thorold to the Great Lakes and therefore hundreds of growing Canadian and American towns.

As canal traffic grew, Thorold established a vibrant pulp and paper industry, shipping paper products throughout the Golden Horseshoe and beyond. Along with industry and freight came a lively banking and lodging district which lined the downtown. With the banks came prosperity. Residences such as the Keefer Mansion were constructed, reported to be the most splendid home this side of Toronto and Rochester.

By the early 1900s, Thorold had developed rich social support structures, including healthcare facilities and the finest educational institutions. In fact, Thorold became widely recognized for its progressiveness in the establishment of educational facilities.

The catalyst for that educational progress was the famous Reverend Egerton Ryerson (1803–1882), the founder of Ontario's public school system, who was among the first Protestant ministers to settle in Thorold. Ryerson believed that social class should not be a roadblock to education and that Canada should have a free and compulsory public education system. Thorold was included in this vision, and local schools were accordingly constructed. Educational boards were constituted. Academic vigour was applied.

As Thorold grew, faith communities also began to dot the landscape. In particular, Baptist, Presbyterian, Anglican, Methodist, Catholic, and United congregations took root. Each week groups of parishioners gathered downtown in their respective new buildings of limestone, Italian blue-veined marble, and onyx.

Thorold was a Christian community. In fact, faith and living out the gospel was at the heart of its people's communal life. Abundant local records highlight the faith communities gathering and worshiping together. Accounts go as far back as the late 1800s of the Catholic pastor Father Lee and Presbyterian minister John William Baynes rallying their churches to worship together at Easter and Christmas services, at which they took offerings to ensure the care of those in need in the city.

Present-day Thorold. In 2019, the city of Thorold boasted a population of 18,801. Today, the architecture in downtown Thorold moans of the affluence that once was. A handful of the magnificent century-old buildings in the neighbourhood now stand derelict or are boarded up. The city is far from the place of economic prosperity it once was.

In some cases, the buildings have been beautifully gentrified with new front entrances and stylish facades. But at the rear of these structures hang rusty back door fire escapes, dangling from low-income housing. Alleyways between buildings bustle not with people and commerce but with darkness, cigarette butts, and discarded syringes.

Inside one apartment is a young family who waits for the sun to come up before moving about the room. Ever since the electricity was cut off (for not paying the bills), they have become accustomed to living without lights. In another building, people lay on thin mats next to piles of junk. Income tax data from 2013 shows that nearly one in four children (twenty-four percent) in the city live in poverty,[92] without suitable food, clothing, or housing.

An old bank lobby is strewn with the homeless. Community Care of St. Catharines & Thorold notes that the number

92   Melinda Cheevers, "Tackling 'Monster of Poverty' in Niagara Region," *Niagara This Week*. September 23, 2016.

of people in their community continues to rise.[93] In the Niagara Region, there are 6,016 households (10,641 individuals)[94] on the waiting list for affordable housing. In Thorold, wait times for affordable housing for low-income families (two-bedroom homes) stand at a whopping eight years, nearly twice the wait of any other community in the region.

Today, Ryerson's vision for educational progress is eclipsed by academic insolvency. Based on academic performance, some schools in Thorold rank in the bottom fifth percentile of educational institutions in Niagara, which overall has more than one hundred fifty schools. Provincially, the report card is just as grim. One Thorold school ranks 2,894th among more than three thousand schools in the province of Ontario.[95] One elementary school in Thorold is continually challenged by dramatic enrollment fluctuations. Every spring, roughly twenty-five percent of students enrolled leave the school to go to another school because their families are evicted from their homes.

Perhaps Ryerson's vision for progressive education in the face of poverty was a prophecy, in a way. Presently, there is more to be told of scholastic poverty than progress in downtown Thorold.

In the back corner of a dark old tavern downtown sits a group of effervescent octogenarians who talk about the way it used to be—not in a general sense, as most of us do, but with more rooted tones. "Thorold *used to be* a good place to work," says one man. "But now all the factories are gone."[96]

---

93   "Donation," *Community Care of St. Catharines & Thorold*. Date of access: January 25, 2021 (https://www.communitycarestca.ca/donation).

94   From a 115-page report about housing and homelessness in the Niagara Region, *A Home for All*. The document can be accessed here: https://www.niagararegion.ca/HHAP

95   Bill Sawchuck, "Report Puts Niagara Schools to the Test," *The Standard*. February 3, 2014.

96   Indeed, an exaggeration.

Local paper mills once pumping out some 197,000 metric tons of newsprint annually now sit idle.[97] A news article in *Niagara This Week* talks about a Thorold auto parts manufacturer closing down, putting more than a hundred people out of work.[98] A local politician calls these industrial shutdowns a "devastating blow to Thorold's economy."[99] The mayor pleads for help: "We're willing to sit down anytime and see what we can do… to get [those] plants going again."[100]

The churches of the past still dot the city today. Some are vibrant churches with amazing leadership. In others, attendance has dwindled to close-to-shuttering lows. Statistics Canada data from 2013 shows that one-third of the Thorold community identifies as Protestant.[101] More pronounced is the Catholic faith, with one-half of the population identifying as such. While statistics suggest church membership remains strong, church engagement is a mere vestige of what it once was. Further statistics show that faith and religious loyalties are dwindling.

97   Karen Walter, "Thorold Mill Idled Indefinitely," *The Standard*. March 10, 2017.

98   "Last of Dana's Jobs Leaving Town," *Niagara This Week*. November 1, 2007 (https://www.niagarathisweek.com/news-story/3293333-last-of-dana-s-jobs-leaving-town/).

99   Paul Forsyth, "Thorold Paper Plant to be Idled," *Niagara This Week*. January 17, 2014.

100 "Thorold Mill Idled Indefinitely," *Niagara Falls Review*. March 10, 2017 (https://www.niagarafallsreview.ca/news/niagara-region/2017/03/10/thorold-mill-idled-indefinitely.html).

101 "Census Profile, 2016 Census: Thorold, City," *Statistics Canada*. Date of access: January 25, 2021 (https://www12.statcan.gc.ca/census-recensement/2016/dp-pd/prof/details/page.cfm?Lang=E&Geo1=CSD&Code1=3526037&Geo2=PR&Code2=35&SearchText=Thorold&SearchType=Begins&SearchPR=01&B1=All&GeoLevel=PR&GeoCode=3526037&TABID=1&type=0).

Observational analysis indicates that Thorold has a dramatically lower number of people associated with religion and faith than the statistics would suggest. The average parishioner in downtown is roughly sixty years old and aging.

Review: Thorold's past and present. By way of review, it has been pointed out that the roots of downtown Thorold's past is characterized by social, economic, academic, and religious prosperity. Yet today downtown Thorold is marked by social, economic, academic, and spiritual poverty.

- Social poverty. Many people live in relational isolation and have a deep longing to connect with their neighbours and develop authentic friendships.
- Economic poverty. Many of our neighbours do not have suitable housing, clothing, and food. Income tax statistics indicate that one in four children (twenty-five percent) in the downtown live in poverty.
- Academic poverty. Academic performance in downtown schools ranks in the bottom fifth percentile of educational institutions of more than one hundred fifty schools in Niagara. Provincially, the report card is just as grim, with at least one school ranking 2,894th of Ontario's three thousand schools. Similarly, most parents in the inner city have a high-school-level education or less.
- Spiritual poverty. People's association with God and the church is dwindling.

Some might call the above analysis a dystopian view of downtown Thorold. I would say it instead defines the reality of downtown Thorold for the purposes of meaningful engagement. It was Max De Pree, a leadership guru, who said that the first responsibility of leaders is to define reality.[102] With these realities in view, we need to ask, are these hard truths what we imagine for our city? Is this what we dream for our community? Better yet, what are going to do about it? Are these realities what early settlers to the Thorold area envisioned long ago?

Perhaps there's a correlation between job loss, poverty, hunger, and bad grades. According to a report in the Niagara Region, "Food insecurity and income are closely linked."[103] Further, reports have shown that children experiencing hunger are more likely to have problems with memory and concentration because they do not have the energy to carry out these functions.[104] This message rings true for many families and their children in downtown Thorold who scrape for their next paycheck while seeking to belong in our culture.

In closing, if you were to walk past Thorold City Hall, you would see hanging there the coat of arms with the words *Cervus non-Servus*. Loosely translated, the words mean "having energy and strength, not willing to give up." It is a tagline which no one person in Thorold today could claim authorship. But that doesn't make it any less true about Thorodites. Thorold residents have incredible energy and strength. And we are never willing to give up. For that reason, we not only long for but expect a new day to dawn in our city.

102   Max De Pree, *Leadership Is an Art* (New York, NY: Currency, 2004).

103   "Niagara Hunger Statistics," *Niagara Region*. Date of access: January 25, 2021 (https://www.niagararegion.ca/living/health_wellness/healthy-eating/hungry/testimonials/hunger-information.aspx).

104   Janice Ke and Elizabeth Lee Ford-Jones, "Food Insecurity and Hunger: A Review of the Effects on Children's Health and Behaviour," *National Center for Biotechnology Information*. March 2015 (https://www.ncbi.nlm.nih.gov/pmc/articles/PMC4373582/).

Bibliography

St. Augustine, Philip Schaff, ed., *The Complete Works of Saint Augustine*.

"Balancing Rhythms of Rest and Work (Overview)," *Theology of Work*. Date of access: January 25, 2021 (https://www.theologyofwork.org/key-topics/rest-and-work-overview).

Beauty and the Beast, directed by Gary Trousdale and Kirk Wise (Los Angeles, CA: Walt Disney Pictures, 1991).

Christopher A. Beeley, *Gregory of Nazianzus on the Trinity and the Knowledge of God* (New York, NY: Oxford University Press, 2008), 255.

Benedict of Nursia, *The Rule of St. Benedict*, trans. Boniface Verheyen, 1949, lvi.

Dietrich Bonhoeffer, "Letter to Eberhard Bethge," *Letters and Papers from Prison*, ed. E. Bethge, trans. Reginald Fuller (New York, NY: Macmillan, 1871), 359–361.

Dietrich Bonhoeffer, *Life Together and Prayerbook of the Bible* (Minneapolis, MN: Fortress Press, 2004), 32.

John Calvin, *Institutes of the Christian Religion* (Peabody, MA: Hendrickson Publisher, 2008), I.iii.

"Census Profile, 2016 Census: Thorold, City," *Statistics Canada*. Date of access: January 25, 2021 (https://www12.statcan.gc.ca/census-recensement/2016/dp-pd/prof/details/

page.cfm?Lang=E&Geo1=CSD&Code1=3526037&-
Geo2=PR&Code2=35&SearchText=Thorold&Search-
Type=Begins&SearchPR=01&B1=All&GeoLevel=PR&-
GeoCode=3526037&TABID=1&type=0).

Melinda Cheevers, "Tackling 'Monster of Poverty' in Niagara Region," *Niagara This Week*. September 23, 2016.

Steven J. Cole, "Broken, but Blessed," *Bible.org*. Date of access: January 18, 2021 (https://bible.org/seriespage/les-
son-59-broken-blessed-genesis-3222-32)

Larry Crabb, *Connecting* (Nashville, TN: W Publishing Group,
1997), 31.

Max De Pree, *Leadership Is an Art* (New York, NY: Currency,
2004).

"Donation," *Community Care of St. Catharines & Thorold*. Date
of access: January 25, 2021 (https://www.communitycar-
estca.ca/donation).

James C. Fenhagen, *Mutual Ministry: New Vitality for the Local
Church* (New York, NY: Seabury Press, 1977), 5.

Paul Forsyth, "Thorold Paper Plant to be Idled," *Niagara This
Week*. January 17, 2014.

Malcolm Gladwell, *The Tipping Point* (New York, NY: Back Bay
Books, 2002), 31–33.

Karen V. Guth, "Claims on Bonhoeffer: The Misuse of a Theologian," *The Christian Century*. May 13, 2015 (https://www.
christiancentury.org/article/2015-05/claims-bonhoeffer).

Simon Carey Holt, *God Next Door: Spirituality & Mission in the
Neighborhood* (Victoria, BC: Acorn Press, 2007), Kindle
location 721.

Heino O. Kadai, "Luther's Theology of the Cross." *Concordia
Theological Quarterly*, July 1999. Quoting Martin Luther.

Janice Ke and Elizabeth Lee Ford-Jones, "Food Insecurity and
Hunger: A Review of the Effects on Children's Health and

Behaviour," *National Center for Biotechnology Information*. March 2015 (https://www.ncbi.nlm.nih.gov/pmc/articles/PMC4373582/).

Tim Keller, *Center Church* (Grand Rapids, MI: Zondervan, 2012), 31.

Hendrik Kraemer, *A Theology of the Laity* (Vancouver, BC: Regent College Publishing, 1958), 83.

"Last of Dana's Jobs Leaving Town," *Niagara This Week*. November 1, 2007 (https://www.niagarathisweek.com/news-story/3293333-last-of-dana-s-jobs-leaving-town/).

"The Lord's Supper," *Heidelberg Catechism*, a church document published by the Christian Reformed Church in 1987 (Grand Rapids, MI).Robert Linthicum, *City of God; City of Satan* (Grand Rapids, MI: Zondervan, 1991), Kindle location 1390.

Martin Luther, *Concerning Christian Liberty* (New York, NY: P.F Collier & Son, 1910), 336–378.

Brian J. Matz, *Re-Reading Gregory of Nazianzus: Essays on History, Theology, and Culture* (Washington, DC: The Catholic University of America Press. 2012), 58.

Alister E. McGrath, *Christian Theology* (Chichester, UK: John Wiley & Sons Ltd., 2017), 297.

"Niagara Hunger Statistics," *Niagara Region*. Date of access: January 25, 2021 (https://www.niagararegion.ca/living/health_wellness/healthyeating/hungry/testimonials/hunger-information.aspx).

Henri Nouwen, *In the Name of Jesus* (Spring Valley, NY: Crossroad Publishing ,1989), 41. Alan Hirsch, "The Spirit of Innovation: Creating New Futures for the Jesus Movement," *The Permanent Revolution* (San Francisco, CA: Jossey-Bass, 2012), 183–204.

Henri Nouwen, "Together We Pray to God." Date of access: January 25, 2021 (https://henrinouwen.org/meditation/together-we-pray-to-god).

Jay Pathak and Dave Runyon, *The Art of Neighboring* (Grand Rapids, MI: Baker Books, 2012), 102.

John Piper, "You Have the Words of Eternal Life," *Desiring God*. December 20, 2009 (https://www.desiringgod.org/messages/you-have-the-words-of-eternal-life).

Cornelius Plantinga Jr., *Not the Way It's Supposed to Be: A Breviary of Sin* (Grand Rapids, MI: Eerdmans, 1995), 10.

"Research About Volunteering in Canada," *Sector Source*. Date of access: January 18, 2021 (http://sectorsource.ca/research-and-impact/volunteering-research).

Paschal Robinson, *The Writings of St. Francis of Assisi*, (Philadelphia, PA: Dolphin Press, 2008), 25–74.

Bill Sawchuck, "Report Puts Niagara Schools to the Test," *The Standard*. February 3, 2014.

Stephen Seamands, *Ministry in the Image of God: The Trinitarian Shape of Christian Service* (Downers Grove, IL: Intervarsity Press, 2005), 41.

John Stott, "Evangelism," *Christian Mission in the Modern World* (Downers Grove, IL: InterVarsity Press, 1975), 38.

"Teresa of Ávila Quotes," *Goodreads*. Date of access: January 25, 2021 (https://www.goodreads.com/quotes/66880-christ-has-no-body-now-but-yours-no-hands-no).

Joel Thiessen, "Episode 6, Part Two," NewLeaf Podcast. June 6, 2018 (https://www.newleafnetwork.ca/podcast/newleaf-project-episode-005-joel-thiessen-part-1), 15:00. Paraphrased.

"Thorold Mill Idled Indefinitely," *Niagara Falls Review*. March 10, 2017 (https://www.niagarafallsreview.ca/news/niagara-region/2017/03/10/thorold-mill-idled-indefinitely.html).

John F. Thoroton and Susan B. Varenne, eds., *Honey and Salt: Selected Spiritual Writings of Bernard of Clairvaux* (New York, NY: Knopf Doubleday, 2007), xvii–li.

Jeff Vanderstelt, *Gospel Fluency* (Wheaton, IL: Crossway, 2017), 3.

Karen Walter, "Thorold Mill Idled Indefinitely," *The Standard*. March 10, 2017.

James Watson, *Religious Nones: A Growing Trend*, New Leaf. April 22, 2017 (https://newleafnetwork.squarespace.com/articles/religious-nones-growing-trend).

John Wesley, *A Plain Account of the People Called Methodists*. An old church document written by John Wesley to Vincent Perronet on December 25, 1748.

Dallas Willard, *The Spirit of the Disciples* (New York, NY: Harper Collins, 1991), 3–5.

Reggie L. Williams, *Black Jesus: Harlem Renaissance Theology and an Ethic of Resistance* (Waco, TX: Baylor University Press, 2014), 200.

J.H. Christopher Wright, *The Mission of God: Unlocking the Bible's Grand Narrative* (Downers Grove, IL: InterVarsity Press, 2006), 23.

About the Author

Terence Schilstra is a missional community leader at The Table, serving among the unreached urban poor in downtown Thorold, Ontario where he lives with his beautiful wife and four children. He has been involved in church planting and missional communities in various capacities for more than a decade. His passion is to cultivate the imagination of the church towards faith and missional engagement in their neighbourhoods. He has a M.Div. from Tyndale Seminary Church-in-the-City program, which forms missional leaders for urban ministry in the twenty-first century.